Liberation

Ntombizodwa Nyoni

methuen | drama

LONDON • NEW YORK • OXFORD • NEW DELHI • SYDNEY

METHUEN DRAMA

Bloomsbury Publishing Plc, 50 Bedford Square, London, WC1B 3DP, UK
Bloomsbury Publishing Inc, 1359 Broadway, New York, NY 10018, USA
Bloomsbury Publishing Ireland, 29 Earlsfort Terrace, Dublin 2,
D02 AY28, Ireland

BLOOMSBURY, METHUEN DRAMA and the Methuen
Drama logo are trademarks of Bloomsbury Publishing Plc.

First published in Great Britain 2025

A catalogue record for this book is available from the British Library.

Library of Congress Control Number: 2025941206

ISBN: PB: 978-1-3505-8646-8
ePDF: 978-1-3505-8647-5
eBook: 978-1-3505-8648-2

Series: Modern Plays

Typeset by Mark Heslington Ltd, Scarborough, North Yorkshire

For product safety related questions contact
productsafety@bloomsbury.com.

To find out more about our authors and books visit
www.bloomsbury.com and sign up for our newsletters.

Liberation

Ntombizodwa Nyoni

Commissioned by the Royal Exchange Theatre
Produced by the Royal Exchange Theatre and
Factory International, Manchester

The first performance of Liberation was at the Royal
Exchange Theatre, Manchester, on 27 June 2025

Liberation
by Ntombizodwa Nyoni

Alma La Badie	**Leonie Elliott**
Kwame Nkrumah	**Eric Kofi Abrefa**
Makumalo Hlubi	**Rudolphe Mdlongwa**
Jomo Kenyatta	**Tonderai Munyevu**
Len Johnson	**Tachia Newall**
Amy Ashwood Garvey	**Pamela Nomvete**
Joe Appiah	**Joshua Roberts-Mensah**
Betty Dorman	**Bex Smith**
Dorothy Pizer	**Nicola Stephenson**
George Padmore	**Eamonn Walker**
WRITER	**Ntombizodwa Nyoni**
DIRECTOR	**Monique Touko**
SET DESIGNER	**Paul Wills**
COSTUME DESIGNER	**Sunny Dolat**
VIDEO DESIGNER	**Dick Straker**
COMPOSER	**Ife Ogunjobi**
LIGHTING DESIGNER	**Matt Haskins**
SOUND DESIGNERS	**Alexandra Faye Braithwaite**
	Nick Lodge
MOVEMENT DIRECTOR	**Kloé Dean**
CONSULTANT DRAMATURG /	
DIRECTOR	**Chinonyerem Odimba**
FIGHT & INTIMACY DIRECTOR	**Bethan Clark**
VOICE & DIALECT COACH	**Joel Trill**
DRAMATHERAPIST	**Samantha Adams**
GROUNDING & SAFE PRACTICE	**Uwarobosa Enobakhare**
ASSOCIATE MOVEMENT DIRECTOR	**Cache Thake**
HODGKISS ASSISTANT DIRECTOR	**Robert Furey**
FACTORY FELLOW	**Stef Reynolds**
CASTING DIRECTOR	**Sophie Parrott CDG**
STAGE MANAGER	**Shannon Aisha Martin**
DEPUTY STAGE MANAGER	**Sarah Barnes**
ASSISTANT STAGE MANAGER	**Joshua Cole-Brown**

New Work Giving Circle Production Sponsor
We are grateful for the support of David Gaskill for his commitment to bringing new works to the stage.

Ntombizodwa Nyoni – Writer

Ntombizodwa Nyoni was on the BIFA mentoring programme and an international fellow on Oxbelly's Episodic Writers Program. Theatre credits include: *The Darkest Part of the Night* (shortlisted for the Alfred Fagon Award & George Devine Award 2021, Kiln Theatre); *Ode to Leeds* (Leeds Playhouse); *Weathered Estates* (City of Culture 2017/ Hull University); *Borderline* (Young Vic); *Nine Lives* (Bridge Theatre, UK Tour); *Boi Boi Is Dead* (finalist for the 2015 Susan Smith Blackburn Prize – Leeds Playhouse, Tiata Fahodzi & Watford Palace Theatre). She is under commission at Bristol Old Vic and The Kiln Theatre. Film/TV credits include: *Castlevania: Nocturne* (S1 & 2, Netflix), and the award winning, *The Ancestors* (BBC Films & BFI Network).

Monique Touko – Director

Monique Touko is a recipient of the 2022 Stage Debut Award for Best Director. Directing credits include: UK premiere of *Marie and Rosetta* (Rose Theatre, and Chichester Festival Theatre); *G* (Royal Court); UK premiere of *Wedding Band: A Love Hate Story in Black and White* (Lyric Hammersmith); *The Boy At The Back of The Class* (National Tour); UK premiere of *School Girls; Or, The African Mean Girls Play* (Lyric Hammersmith); *We Need New Names* (National Tour); *Gone Too Far!* (Theatre Royal Stratford East); *The Clinic* (Almeida Theatre); *Fair Play* (Bush Theatre); *Malindadzimu* (Hampstead Theatre).

Paul Wills – Set Designer

Paul Wills is a critically acclaimed international set and costume designer. Credits include: *Hamlet* (RSC); *The Monstrous Child* (Royal Opera House); *The Clinic* (Almeida Theatre); *Anna Christie, The Cut, The Man Who Had all the Luck* (Donmar Warehouse); *Measure for Measure* (NYC); *King Lear, Fortune, An Enemy of the People* (Tokyo); *Here You Come Again, Shirley Valentine, King Lear, Frozen, American Buffalo, Lady Windermere's Fan, Di and Viv and Rose, Mrs Henderson Presents* (West End); *Romeo & Juliet, The Comedy of Errors, The Tempest, The Four Seasons* (Shakespeare's' Globe); *Wedding Band, School Girls; Or, The African Mean Girls Play, Blasted, Saved; The Lyric. The Acid Test* (Royal Court); *Pig Heart Boy* (Unicorn Theatre); *Les Misérables* (West End, international productions, Arena World / Tour).

Sunny Dolat – Costume Designer

Sunny Dolat is a Kenyan fashion curator and creative director, renowned for his contributions to the international arts and culture scene. With a background in styling and photography, Dolat co-founded the Nest Collective, a multidisciplinary Kenyan group working across film, fashion, visual arts, and music to challenge norms, and dream of new, more equitable realities. In 2016, he published *Not African Enough*, which critiques the stereotypes that have shaped perceptions of African fashion beyond the continent. Dolat was a key member of the curatorial team for the landmark *Africa Fashion* exhibition at the Victoria & Albert Museum in London.

Ife Ogunjobi – Composer

Ife Ogunjobi is a London raised musician born to Nigerian parents whose music is an amalgamation of the sounds around his upbringing. Growing up in south-east London, his surroundings have enriched his music with various genres such as jazz, Afrobeat and hip-hop. He has also performed at sold out stadiums like Madison Square Garden with Wizkid and Burna Boy, headlining at London Omeara, and made appearances at Love Supreme and We Out Here. EP credits: *Stay True* (2023). Ife is part of the band Ezra Collective who won the 2023 Mercury Prize for their album *Where I'm Meant to Be*.

Matt Haskins – Lighting Designer

Matt Haskins' theatre credits include: *Hobson's Choice, Crocodiles* (Royal Exchange Theatre); *A Tupperware of Ashes* (National Theatre); *The Empress* (RSC); *Peter Pan Goes Wrong* (West End & Broadway); *Jesus Christ Superstar, Miss Saigon* (Folketeateret Oslo); *The Clinic* (Almeida); *Marie & Rosetta* (Rose/Chichester); *School Girls; or, The African Mean Girls Play, The Wedding Band* (Lyric Hammersmith); *Fair Play* (Bush); *A Thousand Splendid Suns, The Lovely Bones* (Birmingham Rep); *Girls & Boys, Private Peaceful* (Nottingham Playhouse); *The Girls of Slender Means* (Edinburgh Lyceum); *I and You, Fever Syndrome, Mary, Cost of Living* (Hampstead); *Wish You Were Here* (Gate).

Dick Straker – Video Designer

Dick Straker is a Video and Projection Designer and the founder of Mesmer. Theatre and opera credits include: *Becoming Nancy* (Birmingham Rep); *Rusalka* (ORW, Belgium); *The Pillowman* (Duke of York); *Notorious* (Gothenburg Opera); *Cymbeline* (RSC); *The Ring Cycle* (ROH); *Hitchcock Blonde* (Royal Court); *Julius Ceasar* (The Barbican); *The Woman in White* (Palace Theatre); *The Coast of Utopia, Jumpers* (National Theatre); *Riverdance* (Point Theatre, 1995). Dick has designed for fashion, commercial and architectural project events including projection design for Alexander McQueen's Savage Beauty exhibitions. He formed the company Mesmer in 1993.

Alexandra Faye Braithwaite – Sound Designer

Alexandra Faye Braithwaite's theatre credits include: *Giant, Sound of the Underground, Purple Snowflakes and Titty Wanks* (Royal Court); *Underdog: The Other Other Brontë* (National Theatre); *The Real Thing* (Old Vic); *Punch* (Nottingham Playhouse/Young Vic/Apollo Theatre/Samuel J Freidman Theatre); *Falkland Sound* (Royal Shakespeare Company); *A Taste of Honey, Cat on a Hot Tin Roof, Wuthering Heights, Light Falls* (Royal Exchange Theatre); *Chariots of Fire, Anna Karenina, Operation Crucible, Chicken Soup* (Sheffield Theatres); *The Good Person of Szechwan* (Lyric Hammersmith/Sheffield Theatres); *Bloody Elle* (Lyric Theatre/Traverse Theatre/Royal Exchange); *Never Have I Ever, The Narcissist* (Chichester Festival Theatre); *The Creakers* (Southbank Centre/Theatre Royal Plymouth).

Nick Lodge – Sound Designer

Nick Lodge trained at the Liverpool Institute for Performing Arts. Nick is currently working on *The Sound Of Music* (Curve Theatre). Sound designer credits include: *Spend Spend Spend* (Royal Exchange Theatre); *Nine In Concert* (Lowry – Hope Mill) and *Goldilocks and the Three Bears* (Hull New Theatre, Crossroads Pantomimes). Associate sound credits include: *The Bodyguard* (UK Tour); *Barnum* (The Watermill); *2:22* (Gielgud Theatre & UK Tour); *Grease* (UK Tour); *The Addams Family* (London Palladium & UK Tour); *Oliver!* (Leeds Playhouse); *Time Traveller's Wife* (Apollo Theatre); and *The Wizard of Oz* (Icon of the Seas).

Kloé Dean – Movement Director

Kloé Dean is a Choreographer, Movement Director and Performing Artist. Kloé has worked with a range of music artists such as Nao, Little Simz, SAULT, Anne-Marie, Little Mix, Cleo Sol, Ghetts, Nathan Dawe, Ezra Collective and Kojey Radical. Kloé has also worked alongside brands such as Jimmy Choo, Nike, George at ASDA, Marks & Spencer's and Yazoo. Kloé has presented a range of dance theatre and movement direction including the UK premiere of *Marie & Rosetta* staring Beverly Knight (UK Tour); *Our Mighty Groove* (the grand opening of Sadlers Wells East); *(G)ully* (The Royal Court); *Coming To England* (UK Tour); *Tambo and Bones* (Stratford East).

Chinonyerem Odimba – Consultant Dramaturg / Director

Chinonyerem Odimba is a Nigerian-born, British playwright, librettist, screenwriter, director and poet. Chinonyerem is currently the Artistic Director and Chief Executive of tiata fahodzi and an Associate Member of SOLT. Awards include: WGGB Writer's Guild Award winner (2022) for Best Musical Bookwriting for her play *Black Love*, and a finalist for the inaugural Women Playwriting Prize 2020 for her play *Paradise Street*. Theatre credits include: *The Bird Woman of Lewisham* (the Arcola); *Rainy Season*, *His Name is Ishmael* (Bristol Old Vic); *Joanne* (Clean Break); *Amongst the Reeds* (Clean Break/ The Yard Theatre); *Twist* (Theatre Centre); *Sweetness of a Sting* (National Theatre Connections).

Bethan Clark – Fight and Intimacy Director

Bethan Clark's credits include: *Marie and Rosetta* (Rose Theatre, Chichester & ETT); *A Streetcar Named Desire* (Sheffield Crucible); *Inside No.9: Stage/Fight* (Wyndham's); *Princess Essex* (Shakespeare's Globe); *Ghosts, Our Country's Good, Wedding Band: A Love/Hate Story in Black and White* (Lyric Hammersmith); *The Hot Wing King* (National Theatre); *Cowbois* (RSC); *Coram Boy* (Chichester); *Brassed Off* (Theatre by the Lake, SJT & Bolton Octagon); *The Swell* (Orange Tree); *The Prince* (Southwark Playhouse); *A View from the Bridge* (York Theatre Royal); *Dixon and Daughters* (Clean Break & National Theatre); *As You Like It* (Northern Broadsides); *Lord of the Flies* (Theatr Clwyd & Sherman); *Othello* (Liverpool Everyman).

Joel Trill – Voice & Dialect Coach

Joel Trill's theatre credits include: *Mountaintop* (Lyceum Theatre); *Marie and Rosetta* (The Rose Theatre/ Chichester Festival Theatre); *Shifters* (The Duke of York's Theatre); *Play On* (Talawa Theatre); *Wedding Band* (Lyric Hammersmith); *Corum Boy* (Chichester Festival Theatre); *Shifters* (The Bush Theatre); *Beautiful Thing* (Leeds Playhouse / HOME) and *Tambo & Bones* (Stratford East). Screen credits include: *Inheritance* (Sky); *Here We Go Again*; *Mr Loverman*, *Call the Midwife* and *Murder is Easy* (BBC); *The Crown and Queen Charlotte* (Netflix). Film credits include: *A Real Pain*; *Borges & Me*; *Drift*; *My Name is Leon*; *Empire*; *The Ancestors*.

Sophie Parrott CDG – Casting Director

Sophie Parrott CDG's theatre credits include: *Faith Healer, Wedding Band* (Lyric Hammersmith); *The Boy at the Back of the Class* (Rose, Kingston and Tour); *Nora: A Dolls House* (Young Vic); *The Crucible, Buggy Baby, This Beautiful Future* (Yard Theatre); *One Night In Miami, Shebeen, Wonderland* (Nottingham Playhouse); *All The President's Men* (National Theatre); *Death of A Salesman* (Royal & Derngate); *Wish List, Yen* (Royal Court/ Royal Exchange Theatre); *Amsterdam* (ATC); *Rust* (Bush Theatre); *Blood Knot* (Orange Tree Theatre); *The Crocodile* (MIF); *Our Lady of Blundellsands, Sweeney Todd, Othello* (Liverpool Everyman). Television includes: *Call The Midwife* (Series 9–12, 14 &15, Neal Street) and *The House Across The Street* (Clapperboard / Chapter One).

Leonie Elliot – Alma La Badie

Leonie Elliott is a British actress who is best known for starring as series regular 'Lucille Anderson' in BBC1's hit television show *Call The Midwife*. Television credits include: *Eastenders* (BBC1); *Scotch Bonnet, Killed by My Debt* (BBC3); Holby City, Casualty, *Damned* (S2, BBC); *Danny and the Human Zoo* (Red Productions); *Black Mirror: Hated In The Nation* (Netflix). Theatre credits include: *Small Island* (National Theatre); *The Lion King* (The Lyceum Theatre).

Eric Kofi Abrefa – Kwame Nkrumah

Eric Kofi Abrefa's theatre credits include: *Julie, The Amen Corner* (National Theatre); *One Love: Bob Marley Musical* (Birmingham Rep);

Labrinth (Hampstead Theatre); *The Glass Menagerie* (Headlong Productions); *A Taste of Honey* (National Theatre); *Wildfire* (Hampstead Theatre); *Choir Boy* (Royal Court Theatre); *The Sluts of Sutton Drive* (Finborough Theatre). Television credits include: *Supacell* (Netflix); *The One* (Studio Canal); *Harlots* (Monumental Pictures & Hulu); *Informer* (BBC & Amazon); *King Lear* (Amazon); *Deep State* (Fox Networks Group); Jack Ryan (Paramount Television); *Humans* (Series 2, Kudos for Channel 4 / AMC). Film credits include: *The Book of Clarence* (Legendary); *Blue Story* (BBC Films).

Rudolphe Mdlongwa – Makumalo Hlubi

Rudolphe Mdlongwa trained at Bristol Old Vic Theatre School and most recently played the standout role of Okot in the award-winning production of *The Jungle* at St Ann's Warehouse, Brooklyn. His theatre credits include: *Is God Is* (Royal Court); *Barbershop Chronicles* (UK Tour); *The Convert* (Young Vic); *No One Is Coming To Save You* (The Edinburgh Festival Fringe). On screen, Rudolphe has appeared in Doctors (BBC Studios) and in the film *Crews* (Pen Studios).

Tonderai Munyevu – Jomo Kenyatta

Tonderai Munyevu's theatre credits include: *As You Like It* (Shakespeare's Globe); *Mugabe, My Dad and Me* (York Theatre Royal / ETT / Brixton House); *The Claim* (Shoreditch Town Hall); *Precipice* (Grange Festival); *846 Live* (Theatre Royal Stratford East); *Sizwe Banzi Is Dead* (Young Vic); *Black Men Walking* (Royal Court). Television credits include: *Doctors (BBC).* Film credits include: *The Day of the Triffids* (BBC/HBO); and *Something Nice From London* (Latimer). Tonderai is an award-winning writer and director. His creative credits include *Mansfield Park* (Watermill Theatre); *Mugabe, My Dad and Me* (York Theatre Royal / ETT); *The Moors* (Tara Arts).

Tachia Newall – Len Johnson

Tachia Newall's theatre credits include: *Macbeth, Animal Farm* (Leeds Playhouse, UK tour); *Light Falls, Mother Courage and Her Children, Scuttlers, Hamlet* (Royal Exchange Theatre); *Sylvia* (Old Vic); *Love of the Fireflies* (HOME). Television credits include: *Doctor Who* (Disney+); *Pennyworth* (S3, DC/HBO); *Dodger* (Universal

International Studios); *Life After Life* (House Productions); *Silent Witness* (Series 21)*; From Darkness, Casualty, Young Dracula, Doctors* (BBC); *Vera* (Series 5); *Coronation Street* (ITV); *Scott and Bailey* (Red Productions); *Waterloo Road* (Shed Productions); *Moving on* (LA Productions). Film credits include: *Dune* (Legendary Entertainment / Warner Bros.); *Dirty God* (Emu Films & Viking Films).

Pamela Nomvete – Amy Ashwood Garvey

Pamela Nomvete's theatre credits include: *Skeleton Crew* (Donmar Warehouse); *Coriolanus, Comedy Of Errors, Welcome To Thebes* (National Theare); *To Kill A Mockingbird* (Gielgud Theatre); *The Doctor, They Drink It In The Congo* (Almeida Theatre); *Meet Me At Dawn* (Market Theatre Johannesburg); *The Convert* (Young Vic); *Salvation* (national tour); *Nothing But the Truth* (Market Theatre). Film credits include: *The Man in My Basement* (B.O.B. Filmhouse/Protagonist Pictures); *Kingmakers* (Foughtnight Productions); *The Special Relationship* (Rainmark Films, HBO); *Zulu Love Letter* (Natives At Large). Television credits include: *Nightsleeper* (BBC); *Without Sin* (Left Bank Pictures/ITV); *Gangs of London* (S1-S2, Sky Atlantic).

Joshua Roberts-Mensah – Joe Appiah

Joshua Roberts-Mensah is a British-Ghanaian actor and recording artist from south London. Having played a number of characters in the award-winning audio drama *Dem Times* (Spotify), and in the award-winning theatre production *Drum* (Omnibus, New Diorama & Edinburgh Fringe), Joshua is driven by performance as a primary means of expression. Music consultancy for: *For Black Boys Who Have Considered Suicide When the Hue Gets Too Heavy* (New Diorama/Royal Court/West End).

Bex Smith – Betty Dorman

Bex Smith is currently a series regular in Series 2 of *The Good Ship Murder* (Channel 5), as well as playing a recurring part in *Coronation Street* (ITV). She can also be seen in *Life, Casualty (*BBC) and *Britania* (Sky). Theatre credits include: *The Social* (Not Too Tame); *A Midsummer Night's Dream* (Shakespeare North Playhouse) and *Othello* (Frantic Assembly). She is currently working as an Associate Director at the National Youth Theatre.

Nicola Stephenson – Dorothy Pizer

Nicola Stephenson is a prolific actor who first came to prominence in Channel 4's groundbreaking *Brookside*. She has since played iconic roles in many national classics such as *Holby, Emmerdale, Clocking Off* and *Waterloo Road*, as well as critically acclaimed shows such as *Safe House* and *Homefront*. Most recent television work includes ITV dramas *The Long Shadow, Maternal* and *The Walk-In.* Nicola is an excellent stage actor starring in numerous productions in the West End, RSC and National Theatre. Nicola recently performed in *Our Country's Good* at The Lyric Hammersmith and will next be on screen in ITV's highly anticipated, *The Hack.*

Eamonn Walker – George Padmore

Eamonn Walker's theatre credits include: *Othello* (The Globe); *Julius Ceasar* (Belasco Theatre); *Danny & The Deep Blue Sea* (Flipside Productions); *Punchbag* (Hampstead Theatre); *The Housekeeper, Anthony, Four Horsemen of the Apocalypse* (Citizens Theatre). Television credits include: *Chicago Fire, 17th Precinct, Kings, ER* (NBC); *Strike Back* (HBO); *Moses Jones, One Foot in the Algrave* (BBC); *Justice, Duma* (Warner Bros.). Film credits include: *A Lonely Place to Die* (IFC); *Legacy* (Codeblack); *Blood and Bones, Cadillac Records* (Sony); *The Messenger* (Oscilloscope); *Hate* (Showtime); *Lord of War* (Ascendant Pictures); *Tears of the Sun* (Columbia Pictures); *Once in the Life* (Rysher); *The Fall* (Warner Sisters).

About the Royal Exchange Theatre

Manchester's Royal Exchange Theatre Company transforms the way people see theatre, each other and the world around them. Our historic building was taken over by artists in 1976 and today it is an award-winning cultural charity that produces new theatre in-the-round, in communities, on the road and online.

Exchange remains at the heart of everything we make and do. Our currency is brand new drama and reinvigorated classics, the boldest artists and a company of highly skilled makers – all brought together in an imaginative endeavour to share ideas and experiences with the people of Greater Manchester (and beyond).

The Exchange's unique auditorium is powerfully democratic, a space where audiences and performers meet as equals, entering and exiting through the same doors. It is the inspiration for all we do: inviting everyone to understand the past, engage in today's big questions, collectively imagine a better future and lose themselves in the moment of a great night out.

In 2026 our iconic theatre celebrates 50 years of producing award-winning plays, creating work that is ambitious in ideas, form and scale right in the heart of Manchester's city centre.

royalexchange.co.uk

Executive
Artistic Director/Co-CEO, **Selina Cartmell**
Executive Director (Interim)/Co-CEO, **Chris Stafford**

Registered Charity No. 255424. To donate and find out more visit: royalexchange.co.uk/supportus

Morayo Sodipo, Marketing Manager
Liam Steers, Digital Content Producer
Vicky Wormald, CRM and Audiences Data Manager

Operations
Matthew Clifford, Buildings Manager
Caitlin Conners, Head of Commercial, Hospitality and Events
Christiaan de Villiers, Director of Operations and Commercial Activity
Vistie Marsden, Events Coordinator
Grace Sadiku, IT and Operational Support Technician

Producing
Laura Ainsworth, Production Office Assistant
Olivia Barr, Casting Director (Consultant)
Andy Barry, Associate Director (Interim)
Amy Chandler, Producer
Hester Cox Den, Festival Producer
Martha Ford Tomlinson, Assistant Producer
Scott McDonald, Company Manager
Anna Moutrey, Director of Producing

Production
Grace Bastyan, Lighting Technician
Cat Cameron, Running Wigs, Hair and Make-up
Andrew Croft*, Video Programmer/Engineer
Mark Distin Webster, Joint Head of Lighting
Tracy Dunk, Head of Costume
Rachael Duncan Jones, Wardrobe Maintenance
Annabeth Fearnley*, Costume Assistant
Bridget Fell, Running Wardrobe Manager
Louis Fryman, Sound Technician
Helen Hall, Production Manager
Rosie Holditch*, Costume Assistant
Felicia Jagne, Deputy Head of Costume
Matt Lever, Joint Head of Lighting
Owen Lewis, Head of Sound
Kevin Leach, Head of Technical Stage
Matt Masson, Deputy Head of Sound
Laurie Nuttall*, Costume Cutter/Maker
Holly O'Neill*, Costume Cutter/Maker
Connor Owens, Stage Automation Operator and Technician
Sean Pritchard, Director of Production
Catherine Richardson*, Dresser
Joanna Shepstone, Head of Wigs, Hair and Make Up
Max Schule, Sound Technician
Adam Steed*, Video Programmer
Tom Sutcliffe, Senior Lighting Technician
Antony Walters, Deputy Head of Technical Stage and Automation Operator

Sarah White Head, Costume Cutter
Scenic art by Richard Nutbourne
Scenic Studio*, Sophie Simpson and Keira Lavin
Set construction by Splinter Scenery*
Imogen Walsh*, Running Wigs, Hair and Make-up
Kate Webster*, Costume Assistant
Lucy Woodcock, Costume Hire Facilitator

The Rivals Team
Theresa Fortune, Events and Hospitality Manager
Martha Edwards and Helen Thomason, Hospitality Supervisors

Hospitality Assistants: Aaron Shaw, Ashley O'Brien, Beata Potrzebouska, Beth Edwards, Ethan Rudd, Gareth Smith, Jake Rayner Blair, Jay Ottewell, Jess Gale, Josie Julyan, Julia Rogers, Kacper Potrzebowski, Laura Brunk, Lauren Ellis-Stretch, Lewis Eades, Lola Middleton, Lydia Trench, Molly Crighton, Neve Clark, Oonagh Maclennan, Rachel Zanetti, Romina Duffy, Rosa Gatley, Sedge James, Stella Cohen, Tatana Dubjukova, Tsen Day-Beaver, Vicky Absolon, Vistie James

Visitor Experience
Matt Averall, Operations Support Coordinator
Rachel Davies, Visitor Experience Lead
Sophie Edmunds, Duty Manager
Daniel Hird, Duty Manager (Casual)
Jennifer Hulman, Box Office Coordinator
Vistie James, Duty Manager (Casual)
Niah Mandla, Operations Support Coordinator
Katie Merrick, Operations Support Coordinator
Chris Owen, Duty Manager (Casual)
Mike Seal, Operations Lead
Matthew Warren, Box Office Coordinator

Visitor Experience Coordinators: Clodagh Chapman, Molly Crighton, Amelia Cox, Liam Dodd, Ashley Foster, Maisie Holland, Vistie James Visitor Experience Assistants: Linnae Abraham, Vicky Absolon, Richard Barry, Verity Bate, Anusia Battersby, Lauren Billingsley, Katy Brooks, Hannah Brown, Jazz Burt, Hamish Campbell-Colquhoun, Olivia Chandler, Mika Cholewa, Sara Cocker, Julie Anne Cowen, Amelia Cox, Molly Crighton, Tsen Day-Beaver, Maya Dhokia, Natasha Dutton, Aimee Eggington, Rosa Gatley, Neil Geddes, Lish Glasgow, Amelia Griffiths, Ellie Harrington, Richard Harrison, Amelia Hall, Ioana Hayder, Will Hayes, Jenny Hill, Maisie Holland, Rebecca Johnson, Megan Jones, Fernanda Juarez-Valquez, Josie Julyan, Arran Kemp, Paul Kirkman, Waleria Koba, Ella Laughton, Nai-Kong Leung, Dustin Li, Benjamin Lucas, Chris McKiernon, Alistair McNicol, Phoebe Mycroft, Tony O'Driscoll, Saskia Pay, Kate Piercy, Emilee Prince, Xsara-Sheneille Pryce, Ren Roberts, Adam Rogers, Ayshea Shames, Holly Simpson, Ethan Scott, Rachel Skelton, Marta Szadowska, Jess Telling, Jess Timperley, Caitlyn Vining, Rose

Warburton, Matthew Warren, Esme Watts, Eliott Whittle, Joe Woolf, Mahdi Zadeh

*consultants for this production or freelance staff member

Honorary Associates
Paul Lee (Chairman 1999 – 2015)
Ben Caldwell (Chairman 2015 – 2023)
Armoghan Mohammed (Chairman 2023 – 2025)

Honorary Members
Nicole May, Sally Penni, Jennifer Raffle, Aziz Rashid, Eva Scott, Geoffrey Shindler, Martyn Torevell, Rob Venable-Greaves

Royal Exchange Theatre Supporters

Principal Funders
Arts Council England
GMCA (Greater Manchester
Combined Authority)
The Oglesby Charitable Trust

Corporate Partner
Bruntwood

Corporate Sponsor
Edwardian Hotels
Fumo by San Carlo
Galloways Printers
King Street Townhouse
Levitt Bernstein
Roomzzz
Royal Exchange Flowers Ltd

Principal Corporate Member
Edmundson Electrical

Encore Corporate Member
Mills & Reeve
Ralli Solicitors LLP
Sanderson Weatherall

Associate Corporate Member
5plus Architects
Hotel Indigo

Supporters' Circle
Jason Austin
Ben & Becky Caldwell
Meg & Peter Cooper
John & Penny Early
Mike Edge & Pippa England
Stephen Garratt
Rachel Haugh
Richard & Elaine Johnson
Carole Nash OBE
Nicola Shindler

Platinum Members
John Batley
Mr J Bishop & Mr J Taylor
Sir Robert & Dr Meriel Boyd
Angela Brookes
Paul & Ann Cannings

Sarah Davnall
Mrs V Fletcher
Peter & Judy Folkman
Irene Gray
Roy & Maria Greenwood
Stephen & Arlene Moss
Robin & Mary Taylor
Louisa Taylor
Helen & Phil Wiles

Gold Members
Daniel Bohuslaw
Dan Byrne & Helena Torre Sevillano
Bill Connor
John & Kim Fox
Geoff Holman
Stella Lowe
Donald Mather
Sebastian Taylor
In memory of Tony Hyland

Special Acknowledgements
Arnold & Brenda Bradshaw
The Baker Family Charitable Trust
Susan Hodgkiss CBE & Sally
Hodgkiss
Torevell & Partners

Trusts & Foundations
Ardonagh Community Trust
Backstage Trust
Duchy of Lancaster
The Baring Foundation
The Esmee Fairbairn Foundation
Fenton Arts Trust
Garfield Weston Foundation
The Granada Foundation
The Headley Trust
Jigsaw Homes
Manchester City Council
The Noël Coward Foundation
The Oglesby Charitable Trust
One Manchester
The Rayne Foundation
Theatre Works
The Thistle Trust

Thank you to all of our donors who wish to remain anonymous

Patron HRH The Duke of Edinburgh KG GCVO

About Factory International

Factory International is the organisation behind Manchester International Festival and the city's landmark cultural space, Aviva Studios.

Factory International commissions, produces and presents a year-round programme of original creative work and special events at Aviva Studios, online, and internationally through its network of co-commissioners and partners. It also stages the city-wide Manchester International Festival (MIF) every other year.

MIF is one of the world's leading arts festivals, and the first to be entirely focused on the commissioning and producing of ambitious new work. Staged every two years in Manchester since 2007, the festival invites world-renowned artists from different art forms and backgrounds to create dynamic, innovative and forward-thinking new work in venues and spaces across Greater Manchester. Previous artist include, Björk, Jeremy Deller, Akram Khan, Yayoi Kusama, David Lynch, Wayne McGregor, Steve McQueen, Yoko Ono, Maxine Peake, Skepta, and The xx.

Factory International plays an important role in the lives of Greater Manchester residents, bringing jobs, skills, training and creative opportunities. Through the Factory Academy, Factory International is training the creative workforce of the future, while its pioneering creative engagement and artist development programmes create year-round opportunities for local people to get involved, from participating in flagship commissions to shaping the organisation through involvement in its public forums.

Aviva Studios was designed by the world-leading practice Office for Metropolitan Architecture (OMA), with Ellen van Loon as lead architect – their first major public building in the UK. Its development was led by Manchester City Council, with backing from HM Government and National Lottery funding from Arts Council England.

Factory International is an Arts Council England National Portfolio Organisation.

factoryinternational.org

Executive Creative Director: **KeeHong Low**
Director of Producing & Programme: **Ric Watts**
Executive Producer: **Ruhi Jhunjhunwala**

Liberation

A fictional story inspired by true events at the
5th Pan-African Congress, Manchester, 1945

liberation

NOUN

1. The action of setting someone free from imprisonment, slavery, or oppression; release.

2. Freedom from limits on thought or behaviour.

How Does a Revolution Begin?

Is it loud like an explosion,
Or does it simmer like a pot on the boil?

Is it the last gasp of air on the front line or the birth of a new thought?

Is it found in a man or a woman?
In the old or the young?
Rich or poor?
Educated or illiterate?

Is it crossing the finishing line with arms jubilantly raised in the air,
Or endlessly travelling a road and passing through time?

Characters

Kwame Nkrumah, *36 years old, Ghanaian activist, Joint Secretary of the Congress.*
Alma La Badie, *37 years old, Jamaican social worker, Congress delegate.*
George Padmore, *43 years old, Trinidadian writer, activist, journalist, organiser and Joint Secretary of the Congress.*
Amy Ashwood Garvey, *48 years old, Jamaican Pan-Africanist activist and Congress Chairman.*
Betty Dorman, *27 years old, working-class white Mancunian, Congress Secretary and Kwame* **Nkrumah**'s *close friend.*
Len Johnson, *43 years old, mixed-race Mancunian (Irish/Sierra Leone) former middle-weight boxer.*
Dorothy Pizer, *39 years old, Londoner, working-class anti-racist activist, stenographer and George* **Padmore**'s *partner.*
Jomo Kenyatta, *54 years old, Kenyan anti-colonial activist, Congress delegate and Cosmopolitan maître d'hôtel.*
Joe Appiah, *27 years old, Ghanaian law student, West African Student Union President and Kwame* **Nkrumah**'s *friend.*
Makumalo Hlubi, *28 years old, South African medical student, actor, Congress delegate and Kwame* **Nkrumah**'s *friend.*

Notes

Stage directions are in italics.

/ is an interruption.

. . . delayed response.

Music throughout the play should celebrate the diversity of cultures represented at the Congress.

Act One

DAY 1, MONDAY 15 OCTOBER 1945

Prologue: Call to Arms

Scene One: Welcome To Manchester
Upstairs Gallery, Chorlton-on-Medlock Town Hall. Morning.

Scene Two: It's Alma, Alma La Badie
Upstairs Gallery, Chorlton-on-Medlock Town Hall. Morning.

Congress Speech
Speaker: **Alma La Badie**

Scene Three: Brothers
Nkrumah, **Appiah** *and* **Hlubi**'s *boarding house. Evening.*

Scene Four: Cheers!
Cosmopolitan Club. Late evening.

Congress Speech
Speakers: **George Padmore**, **Kwame Nkrumah**

DAY 2: TUESDAY 16 OCTOBER 1945

Scene Five: Black Man, Black Woman
Boardroom, Chorlton-on-Medlock Town Hall. Afternoon.

Congress Speech
Speaker: **Jomo Kenyatta**

DAY 3: WEDNESDAY 17 OCTOBER 1945

Scene Six: Tactics
Upstairs corridor, Chorlton-on-Medlock Town Hall. Afternoon.

Congress Speech
Speaker: **Makumalo Hlubi**

Scene Seven: Respectability Politics
*Upstairs Gallery, Chorlton-on-Medlock Town Hall. Late
afternoon.*

Act Two

DAY 4: THURSDAY 18 OCTOBER 1945

Scene One: The Gloves Are Off
Cosmopolitan Club. Evening.

DAY 5: FRIDAY 19 OCTOBER 1945

Scene Two: On the Same Team
Pizer *and* **Padmore** *kitchen. Morning.*

Scene Three: Black Woman to Black Woman
All Saints Church Grounds. Afternoon.

Scene Four: Declarations
Forum Restaurant. Afternoon.

Scene Five: Legacy
Forum Restaurant. Afternoon.

Congress Portraits
Chorlton-on-Medlock Town Hall. Evening.

Act One

Prologue

The Call to Arms

George Padmore *enters. He sits at his typewriter. He slides in a piece of paper. His hands hover over the keys. Beat. He starts typing. A projection appears:*

'Press Release No. 4'

Padmore   From the Publicity Department of the Pan-African Federation. Head Office, 58 Oxford Road, Manchester, England. (*Beat.*) This message is for all colonised peoples of the world.

Enter **Kwame Nkrumah** *and* **Alma La Badie** *from opposite directions reading copies of the press release.*

Padmore   In February, at the World Trade Union Conference in London, the Pan-African Federation invited the colonial delegates to join us afterwards for an informal meeting in Manchester.

Enter **Amy Ashwood Garvey** *and* **Jomo Kenyatta** *reading copies of the press release.*

Padmore   I wanted to propose an idea; the planning of a World Pan-African Congress.

Enter **Joe Appiah** *and* **Makumalo Hlubi** *reading copies of the press release.*

Padmore   European imperialism has politically dominated for centuries. For generations, the Empire walls served to keep African, and peoples of African descent divided and uninformed, while capitalism and imperialism thrives.

Enter **Betty Dorman** *and* **Len Johnson** *reading copies of the press release.*

Padmore   The walls have been reduced to rubble. Pathways to each other are open. (*They look at each other. Beat.* **Padmore** *turns to them*.) Time is of the essence.

I desperately urge you to find your critical thinkers, your scholars, your community organisers, your labourers, your teachers, your mothers, your sons. (*Beat*.) Prepare them to mobilise.

They all exit.

This Congress must take place before the year concludes. It must be the greatest and most representative ever called by Africans and people of the African descent.

Enter **Dorothy Pizer**. **Padmore** *continues typing. She hovers over* **Padmore***'s shoulder and reads what he's typing.*

Padmore   Our freedom comes from collective planning and action. (*Beat*.) Further details to follow. (*Beat*.) Yours truly, George Padmore, Co-founder of the Federation.

Pizer *hugs him. Beat. They exit.*

Scene One

Welcome to Manchester

Day 1, 15 October 1945. Morning.

Upstairs Gallery, Chorlton-on-Medlock Town Hall.

Upbeat music plays. A projection appears:

'DAY 1: 15 OCTOBER 1945'

The stage is fully illuminated to reveal hanging posters reading: 'DOWN WITH TRUSTEESHIP', 'DOWN WITH LYNCHING AND JIM CROWISM', 'AFRICA FOR THE AFRICANS', 'ARABS AND JEWS UNITE AGAINST BRITISH IMPERIALISM', 'OPPRESSED PEOPLES OF THE WORLD UNITE', 'FREEDOM OF THE PRESS IN THE COLONIES', 'FREEDOM FOR ALL SUBJECT PEOPLES', 'DOWN WITH

ANTI-SEMITISM' and 'LABOUR WITH A WHITE SKIN CANNOT EMANCIPATE ITSELF WHILE LABOUR WITH BLACK SKIN IS BRANDED'. There's also, a map of the continent of Africa, flags of Haiti, Liberia and Ethiopia.

Enter **Nkrumah** *wearing a suit with a pocket square, carrying a box of programmes. He's followed by* **Dorman**, *who wears a form-fitted patterned dress. She takes a hand full of programmes.* **Padmore**, *also wearing a suit with a pocket square, enters with* **Pizer** *in a checked skirt suit, matching coat and a decorative hat. She takes off her coat and gets to work. They all start distributing programmes to the audience. The delegates enter and the dance of salutations begins.*

Appiah wearing a suit adorned with a kente shawl enters with **Hlubi**, *in a dashiki, smart trousers and a traditional Zulu headband. They approach* **Nkrumah** *and playfight with each other.* **Dorman** *approaches them. She takes* **Nkrumah**'s *programmes and shoos the men away like naughty boys. They watch her walk away. They clock each other staring and laugh.* **Nkrumah** *grabs more programmes for himself,* **Appiah** *and* **Hlubi**. *They hand them out to the audience.*

Ashwood Garvey enters. She's in a checked skirt suit, matching coat and a decorative hat. **Padmore** *respectfully bows to* **Ashwood Garvey** *as if greeting royalty.* **Kenyatta** *enters with a long fur coat draped over his suit. He has a kofi hat, a cane and Maasai flywhisk. He approaches* **Pizer** *and greets her by kissing her hand and up along her arm.* **Padmore** *pulls* **Pizer** *away and playfully squares up to* **Kenyatta**. **Kenyatta** *raises his cane and flywhisk.* **Ashwood Garvey** *and* **Pizer** *huddle together like schoolgirls on a playground watching the brawling boys.* **Kenyatta** *flings off the draped coat. Instead of pouncing on* **Padmore**, *he peacocks. He twirls the cain and swats the whisk.* **Padmore**, **Ashwood Garvey** *and* **Pizer** *laugh.*

Padmore (*to* **Kenyatta**)   The Kenyan showman! (*Beat.*) Jomo, you put the rest of us to shame.

Kenyatta   The revolution will be fashionable!

They gather into groups: **Padmore**, **Ashwood Garvey**, **Kenyatta**
and **Pizer***;* **Appiah**, **Hlubi** *and* **Nkrumah**. **Dorman** *continues
interacting with the audience.* **Padmore** *keeps checking the doors
for other guests.*

Nkrumah (*to* **Appiah** *and* **Hlubi**)   Where were you two last
night? I was setting up until the early hours. I've barely slept.

Hlubi   *Bhudi* ('brother' in Zulu), I told you I couldn't help.
I'm still writing my speeches for the week. Something is
missing.

Nkrumah   And what's your excuse?

Appiah   My terms were clear. Introduce me to Mrs
Ashwood Garvey and I'd help. /

Nkrumah   Clearly, I've been preoccupied.

Appiah   You're the one trying to impress George, not me.
(**Appiah** *straightens his shawl*.) How do I look? /

Nkrumah   Desperate.

Appiah *sucks his teeth. Across the room,* **Johnson** *enters.*
Dorman *hands him a programme.* **Dorman** *is smiling.*

Hlubi   Who's that with Betty?

Nkrumah *and* **Appiah** *turn to watch.*

Nkrumah   I don't know.

Hlubi *and* **Appiah** *whisper into each of* **Nkrumah**'*s ears.*

Hlubi   You know, there'll be plenty eligible bachelors in
Manchester this week.

Appiah   Suave, foreign lotharios new to Betty.

Hlubi   Your window is closing with her, Kwame.

Nkrumah *takes a step away from them. They follow.*

Nkrumah (*sucks his teeth*)   For all we know that man is an
informant sent by the Special Branch to spy on us. /

Appiah   He's a coloured man. /

Nkrumah   The enemy will infiltrate us by any means necessary. We must keep an eye on him.

Dorman *laughs loudly and touches* **Johnson**'s *arm.*

Hlubi (*strokes* **Nkrumah**'s *chest*)   Looks like Betty already has two eyes on him /

Nkrumah   *Nka me!* ('Don't touch me!' in Twi).

Appiah *and* **Hlubi** *laugh.*

Johnson   I thought I knew everyone in this city.

Dorman   I promise they're not that intimidating. Give them a little, 'Y'a'll right, our kid?' and they'll welcome you in.

Johnson *circles the room.* **Nkrumah**, **Appiah** *and* **Hlubi** *approach him.* **Johnson** *gives a nodding greeting. They size him up and walk on.* **Pizer** *pulls* **Padmore** *aside.*

Pizer   George, we should get started.

Padmore   Our guest of honour hasn't arrived.

Pizer   Everybody else is here, my love.

Padmore (*whispers*)   I promised Du Bois would be here.

Pizer   Start, and I'll pop to the office in the tea break to check if any telegrams have arrived. Okay?

He nods. **Padmore** *steps to the mic.*

Padmore (*to the room*)   Ladies and gentlemen, please gather for the opening remarks from our esteemed Congress Chairman, the first wife of the great Marcus Garvey, political activist and champion of women's rights, Amy Ashwood Garvey.

The room erupts in clapping, cheers and stomping. **Ashwood Garvey** *steps to the mic. She is regal and commands respect. The room falls silent.*

Ashwood Garvey   Forty-one days ago, the Second World
War ended. (*Beat.*) Winston Churchill called for all citizens
to do the utmost to rebuild, to ensure that each countryman
has a chance moving forward. (*Beat.*) These words were
transmitted throughout the colonies. I listened and
wondered as to whom he was referring as *his* countrymen.
(*Beat.*) And what was he advocating we rebuild?

Beat.

Violence is ruling the colonies, and the metropole proudly
calls itself our trustees. (*Beat.*) My people, you have known a
forced occupation on your lands, on your bodies, on your
histories for far too long. (*Beat.*) The blood of our kin has
stained many foreign battlefields. They celebrated Victory in
Europe Day in May, but our freedom has not been won.
(*Beat.*) We've been a patient people for too long. This will no
longer stand!

The room cheers in agreement.

The new Labour government won the elections. (*Beat.*) The
victory of the common man in England was meant to be the
victory of all men in the colonies. (*Beat.*) This was supposed
to be the socialist answer to Churchill's Tory imperialism.
(*Beat.*) George wrote to Prime Minister Attlee stating Britain
cannot condemn the imperialism of Germany, Japan and
Italy, while condoning the atrocious actions of its own
government, here and the colonies. (*Beat.*) Our concerns
were met with silence. (*Beat.*) So let me say, what we know is
true (*Beat.*) All imperialism is evil!

The room cheers in agreement.

We are no longer waiting for anyone's allyship. We deserve
change. We deserve freedom of the press. We deserve
education. We deserve self-determination, independence,
equality of civil rights and the total abolition of all forms of
racial discrimination. (*Beat.*) The masses must rise!

Appiah (*calls out*)   *Ozie!*

Nkrumah/Hlubi   *Oza!*

They encourage the room to repeat after them.

Appiah   *Ozie!*

Nkrumah/Hlubi   *Oza!*

Ashwood Garvey   Let's strike now before the ink dries on the history pages. (*Beat.*) To all the speakers in the room, you have a responsibility to represent your countries. (*Beat.*) Share what is happening in your homelands. Make your demands clear. (*Beat. Gestures to* **Padmore**.) Our trusted scribe, Mr Padmore, will edit our manifesto, a call to action against the colonial powers. (*Beat.*) Liberation is in your hands! (*Beat. She chants with a clenched fist in the air.*) Ozie!

All   *Oza!*

Ashwood Garvey (*gesturing to the audience*)   *Ozie!*

All   *Oza!*

Ashwood Garvey (*gesturing to the audience*)   *Ozie!*

All   *Oza!*

Ashwood Garvey   Rise!

The room is energised.

Appiah (*to* **Hlubi** *and* **Nkrumah**)   She's incredible.

Ashwood Garvey   Jomo, I hear you are the maître d' at the best drinking hole in Manchester.

Kenyatta   The Cosmopolitan lives in the shadows of the Florence Mills Parlour.

Ashwood Garvey   My landlady days are long behind me. But we must raise a glass for those the Colonial Office blocked from attending.

Kenyatta   Happily /

Padmore   But first, we work.

The room starts to disperse. **Dorman** *approaches* **Nkrumah**.

Dorman (*to* **Nkrumah**)   Hiya, what did George say about the manifesto?

Nkrumah   I haven't asked him yet.

Padmore *approaches* **Nkrumah** *and* **Dorman**.

Padmore   Nkrumah, Betty, come. (*They huddle together.*) We must keep to schedule this week.

Dorman   I've given everyone their orders. Already sent the Entertainment Committee to start on lunches. I also brought extra pens and notebooks from the office.

Padmore   Good, good. I don't want to wait until after the Congress to start drafting the manifesto. There are ten speakers today. I want all rapporteurs to get their summary notes to me at the end of every day.

Dorman   I'll let them know.

Padmore *turns to leave.* **Dorman** *nudges* **Nkrumah**.

Nkrumah (*clears his throat*)   George, if you need help with the manifesto, I'd be happy to transcribe the notes, or hear your initial thoughts. Maybe even, co-edit sections, with your guidance of course.

Padmore (*pats* **Nkrumah** *on the back*)   Nkrumah, focus on your speeches for now. We'll talk later. /

Padmore *turns to exit.*

Nkrumah   Yeah, sure, sure. Thanks, George.

Padmore (*turns back*)   And don't leave your notebooks lying around. The press could be lurking in the crowd. They'll use anything to discredit us.

Padmore *exits leaving* **Nkrumah** *and* **Dorman** *alone on stage. Beat.*

Dorman   He didn't say no.

Nkrumah   He didn't say yes either.

Dorman   George is protective over his writing.

Nkrumah   I've been his mentee for months now Betty. I've studied his writing. Test me, you won't be able to see where he ends, and I begin.

Dorman   You don't have to convince me, Kwame. I know you're a great speaker. But George likes actions. (*Steps closer to him and touches his arm.*) Show him you're ready to be a leader.

She smiles at him. Beat.

Scene Two

It's Alma, Alma La Badie

Day 1: 15 October 1945, morning.

Upstairs Gallery, Chorlton-on-Medlock Town Hall.

Alma La Badie *rushes in carrying her suitcase. She's been rained on. Her entrance disturbs* **Dorman** *and* **Nkrumah**'s *private moment.* **La Badie** *is disappointed to see the room has cleared.*

La Badie   Have I missed it? (*Beat.*) Have I missed Mrs Garvey?

Nkrumah *steps away from* **Dorman**.

Nkrumah   Yes, only by a few minutes.

She drops her suitcase.

La Badie   Dammit! (*Takes off her hat and dries herself.*) The stupid bus driver was chatting to every passenger like he didn't have a schedule to keep. Someone said it would be quicker for me to get off the bus and walk down Oxford Road.

Nkrumah   But I bet they never said the road was longer than a Pentecostal church service.

La Badie   I felt like the Israelites dragging my case in the rain through the wilderness for forty years. I walked past here so many times. Why does every damn building in this country look the same?

Dorman   Welcome to Manchester.

La Badie *doesn't respond to her.*

La Badie   Running up the stairs messed up my dress.

Nkrumah   You still look mighty fine.

Dorman *cuts in.*

Dorman   Best not to dry off completely. The meeting point for volunteers is the Forum Restaurant. It's back up the road. I'll get you a programme. Address is on the back. You'll report to Ras Makonnen.

Dorman *holds out a programme.* **La Badie** *doesn't take it. She steps away and checks out the room. They watch her.*

La Badie (*to* **Dorman**)   You two volunteers?

Dorman   I'm the Congress Secretary. Kwame here, organised the week.

La Badie *speaks into the mic.*

La Badie   I thought Mr George Padmore was the organiser?

Nkrumah   We're on the planning committee together.

Dorman   He's also the Joint Secretary of the Congress.

La Badie *continues pacing around the room.*

La Badie   I hear these gatherings can be quite the boys' club.

Dorman   Amy is here.

La Badie   *Mrs* Ashwood Garvey is a formidable woman, but even she can't speak for all of us.

Nkrumah *steps closer to* **La Badie**. **Dorman** *shadows him.*

Nkrumah   Anyone that can handle being married to the monumental Marcus Garvey, can hold their own anywhere.

La Badie   There's only so much one should hold in this unfair world.

Nkrumah   It's unfair to us all, that's why we're all here, right?

Dorman   That's right. (*Beat.* **La Badie** *doesn't respond to her. She keeps her eyes on* **Nkrumah**. **Dorman** *interjects.*) You should get going. (*She slides the programme into* **La Badie**'s *handbag.*) Lots of lunches to make.

La Badie *puts her hat on and gathers her things.*

La Badie   I need to freshen up. /

Dorman   Why? You're just going to get mucky again. /

La Badie (*to* **Nkrumah**)   Point me to the lavatory, please.

Nkrumah   Down the corridor to the left.

Dorman   And come back here, I need to sign you in before you go.

La Badie *turns to leave.*

Nkrumah   What's your name?

Beat. She turns back.

La Badie   Alma. (*Beat.*) Alma La Badie.

Nkrumah *watches her exit.* **Dorman** *notices.*

Dorman   Did you see how she got on the stage? George won't like that. We don't need any troublemakers this week.

Beat.

Nkrumah   No.

Beat.

Dorman   You should get going too. Get your notes to George before he has a chance to ask you for them.

Nkrumah   You're right. See you later, Betty.

They exit in opposite directions.

Congress Speech

Music plays. **Pizer, Kenyatta, Padmore** *and* **Johnson** *enter.* **La Badie** *steps to the mic.*

La Badie (*to the audience*)   I urge the Congress to consider what happens to the children left behind by coloured American troops and born to married English women, whose husbands were serving overseas. (*Beat.*) Forgiveness doesn't reside in many of these homes. Coloured children are sent away to orphanages. I work at one in Liverpool. These places are in a degraded state, no condition for a child to grow up in; to thrive in. (*Beat.*) Money is needed to care for *our* next generation.

They applaud and exit.

Scene Three

Brothers

Day 1: 15 October 1945, evening.

Nkrumah, Appiah *and* **Hlubi**'*s boarding house.*

The music continues. **Appiah** *and* **Hlubi** *enter, followed by* **Nkrumah** *whose face is in his notebook.* **Appiah** *and* **Hlubi** *pull out their cases and start getting changed.* **Nkrumah** *continues making notes.* **Appiah** *snatches* **Nkrumah**'*s book and tosses it on the bed.*

Appiah   Clock out, Kwame, no one is giving an exam. /

Nkrumah   George might as well be. He likes his notes a certain way.

Hlubi   I hope you're not wearing that shirt to the club. (*Gestures to his suitcase.*) Hurry up, pick something in my case, I don't want all the ladies to be gone by the time we get to the Cosmopolitan.

Nkrumah   They're not a buffet.

Nkrumah *rummages through the suitcases.* **Hlubi**'s *clothing is not his style. He picks a shirt from* **Appiah**'s *clothes.*

Hlubi   There's one or two I'd like to eat.

Appiah (*to* **Nkrumah**)   You should buy Betty a drink tonight. /

Nkrumah   I don't drink. /

Hlubi   She drinks /

Appiah   and dances /

Hlubi   And that's all that matters tonight.

Nkrumah   I'm not staying out late tonight. I need to practice my speech for tomorrow. /

Appiah   Plenty people going out tonight are speaking too. You're not the only one /

Nkrumah (*to* **Appiah**)   You're not. /

Hlubi (*to* **Nkrumah**)   But I am, and I'll be drinking, and dancing, and kissing all night long.

Appiah (*to* **Nkrumah**)   You need to cash in on all those months of sexual tension with Betty /

Nkrumah   Betty and I are friends /

Hlubi   It is a scientific fact. Men and women can never be friends.

Appiah   I want to be Amy's friend.

Nkrumah   She's practically your aunty.

Hlubi   And pheromones attract each other. No matter how platonic you claim to be, one of you is secretly waiting for the opportunity for sex to present itself. /

Nkrumah   That's not true! Betty is my confidant. I'd never want to lose that.

Hlubi   You can't fool me, Kwame. I see what you're doing.

Nkrumah   What am I doing?

Hlubi   You're delaying your orgasm so when it erupts, you'll be an untamed beast writhing in the forest of Betty's screaming desire. (*Mimics* **Dorman**.) Kwame, take me!

Hlubi *dramatically collapses.*

Nkrumah   Not every interaction with the opposite sex must satisfy a hankering, Marko.

Hlubi *and* **Appiah** *exchange perplexed looks.*

Hlubi   Did – did he just say hankering, Joe?

Appiah   Yes, Marko. I think he did.

Nkrumah   For the dumb ones in the room, it means to desire too long for something.

Hlubi *crawls seductively to* **Nkrumah**.

Hlubi   Betty is certainly desiring something loooong.

Nkrumah *runs away.*

Nkrumah (*sucks his teeth*)   There's something wrong with you. /

Hlubi *laughs.*

Appiah   I've seen it in the changing rooms, Marko. His penis is not that long. /

Nkrumah   *Woboa!* ('You're lying' in Twi.) Tell the truth and shame the devil! /

Appiah   *Mekaa nokware.* ('I told the truth' in Twi.) /

Hlubi   Let me see it /

Nkrumah   No /

Hlubi   I'm a medical student, I know what average looks like /

Nkrumah   You quit your studies eight years ago. /

Hlubi   I took a sabbatical for my film debut.

Nkrumah (*mockingly*)   Oh yes, remind me again, who did you play in King Solomon's Mines? (*Beat.*) Dying Kukuanaland Native Number 1? /

Hlubi   I was a named character! /

Nkrumah   A named prop is still a prop /

Hlubi   The Sun Never Sets, Harlem in Mayfair, Dark Sophistication. My credits speak for themselves /

Appiah (*to* **Hlubi**)   You don't have to justify yourself, Marko. He's trying to distract us from his impotence.

Nkrumah   I am very, *very* virile /

Appiah   Brew him a herbal concoction, Marko, it'll cure his performance anxiety. /

Nkrumah   My love making is poetic. /

Hlubi   A very short poem /

Hlubi *and* **Appiah** *laugh.* **Nkrumah** *sucks his teeth.*

Nkrumah   Make your jokes, but history will remember me as one of the greats /

Appiah   Of course, you're George's puppy now. /

Nkrumah   Protégé /

Appiah   Errand boy /

Nkrumah   Successor. /

Appiah   You lick a few stamps and now you think you're in line to become the next great revolutionary leader?

Nkrumah   I will be carved into stone like Mount Rushmore.

Appiah   Your delusion is unmatched.

Nkrumah   Jealousy doesn't suit you, my friend. /

Appiah   I am a qualified lawyer. /

Nkrumah   Trainee /

Appiah   That can still sniff out your bullshit, *Francis*. /

Nkrumah   *Ka wano tum!* ('Shut up' in Twi) You know I go by Kwame now /

Appiah   Oh yes, ladies and gentlemen, since making the pilgrimage to meet George Padmore in London nine months ago, Francis has now reinvented himself as an African /

Nkrumah   I have always been an African! I'm just no longer using my English name.

Hlubi   Removing your English name doesn't decolonise that big forehead of yours, Kwame. You still must figure out the man behind the name.

Nkrumah   Isn't that why we are all here?

Hlubi   No, I came for the women and free food. /

Appiah   Get a real job, Marko. /

Nkrumah   Don't listen to him, you're a star my boy. /

Hlubi   Thanks, papa.

Appiah   Idiots. (*Beat.*) Tell me, Kwame, does your purpose here include returning to your PhD studies in London, or are you rejecting that institution too?

Nkrumah   Joe, I left my father back in Half Assini, mind your business.

Appiah   Your supervisor came to me asking if you'd gone to liberate Africa yet. I said I hadn't seen you.

Hlubi   You should have told him the only thing he was liberating were Eccles cakes from their packaging in Manchester. (**Hlubi** *pats* **Nkrumah**'s *stomach*.) Uncle.

Nkrumah (*kisses his teeth*)   The white man's university is not built to elevate an African's mind. (*Beat.*) The LSE wants to dictate how I should spend my money and my time. I want to study the political philosophy of my people. Dr Ayer doesn't want to supervise that. He says I don't have an analytical mind. But my thesis would send questions straight up the hierarchy, through the Chancellor's office, into Downing Street and force the monarchy to confront its genocides.

Appiah   Only you would presume to have the loaded thesis in the gun of liberation before you've even written a single word.

Nkrumah   I am an African in this world, Joe. My life is documentation enough. (*Beat.*) I will not help the university shape me into a poor imitation of a white man.

Appiah   I'm still enrolled in Law School, so by your assertion, I am a mimicry of whiteness /

Nkrumah (*to* **Hlubi**)   Marko, did I say that? /

Hlubi (*exasperated*)   Please don't drag me into your arguments again. You're both as self-centred as each other /

Appiah/Nkrumah   I am nothing like him. /

Hlubi   Political debates are not the only ways to find answers for liberation. There is no freedom without the thespians, the musicians, the painters, the dancers. I contribute to the fight too /

Nkrumah   Then I expect you to dance for me when the enemy surrenders to the first Akan president of the Gold Coast /

Appiah   Great men of all tribes can lead our country to independence. /

Nkrumah   Yes, but I am the one working with George to edit the blueprint for Africa's decolonization. /

Hlubi   Wait, is George letting you edit the manifesto?

Beat.

Nkrumah   George trusts me. (*Beat.*) He respects my voice. He likes my passion.

Hlubi   Dictators have passion too. It doesn't make them good leaders.

Appiah   I'm going to run as the first Asante president of the Gold Coast /

Nkrumah *laughs.*

Nkrumah   You have all the charisma of a grandmother's used waist cloth. (*Beat.*) Our biggest and most ignored voting demographic is the youth. They need someone who can electrify them to revolt. If building anew from the rubble is good enough for British patriotism, it should be the same for black liberation.

Appiah   We must also take control of the economic and legal powers in the colonies first. /

Nkrumah   Revolution, Joe! (**Nkrumah** *pushes* **Appiah** *out of the way.*) Act now!

Appiah   *Firi me so!* ('Get off me!' in Twi.)

Nkrumah *laughs and puts him in a headlock.*

Nkrumah   Don't worry Joe, I will make you a minister, of sanitation for all the shit you talk. /

Hlubi *jumps onto the bed.*

Hlubi (*recites*)   Like Romeo and Mercutio, Antonio and Bassanio, Hamlet and Horatio,

They stop fighting.

Appiah (*to* **Nkrumah**)   What is he doing?

Hlubi (*recites*)   Proteus and Valentine.

Nkrumah (*to* **Appiah**)   Freeing us with his art.

Hlubi (*recites*)   Shaka Zulu and Mzilikazi. Many have philosophised its complex nature. (*Beat.*) But none has said more poetically than Seneca's letters. (*Beat.*) Test a man's character before accepting him as a friend. When you do, welcome him into your heart and soul, speak to him as you would with yourself. (*Beat.*) For true friendships are worth dying for /

Appiah (*to* **Nkrumah**)   I would never die for you.

Nkrumah (*to* **Appiah**)   Agreed /

Hlubi   You two have the kind of friendship you give children namesake to.

Appiah   My lineage will never carry the Kwame name.

Nkrumah (*to* **Appiah**)   Do you know who else were friends?

Appiah   Who?

Beat.

Nkrumah   Jesus and Judas.

Appiah   And who is Judas in this scenario?

Nkrumah   If you must ask.

Appiah *tries to hit* **Nkrumah**.

Appiah   You are not the messiah.

Nkrumah *blocks the hit. He tries to put him in a headlock.*

Nkrumah   You shall be defeated Judas!

Appiah   Let me go!

They tussle.

Hlubi   I give up! *Asambeni!* ('Let's go' in Zulu.) The women are waiting.

Scene Four

Cheers!

Day 1: 15 October 1945, late evening.

Cosmopolitan Club.

Upbeat, electrifying and feverish music plays. A bright 'COSMOPOLITAN' sign hangs above the bar. **Padmore** *nurses a drink at the bar. The delegates dance around him.* **Nkrumah** *and* **Dorman** *dance closely.* **Appiah** *and* **Hlubi** *cheer him on.* **Kenyatta** *meanders around them.*

Kenyatta (*he moans and sways to the music; to the audience*) You like that don't you? (*Beat.*) You like the way the music seduces you? (*Beat.*) The way the sweet liqueur licks your lips. (*Beat.*) The way it smoothly slides your inhibitions off like a satin petticoat. (*Beat.*) OOOOooo you look so sexy. So sharp! So delicious!

Padmore   Keep it clean, Jomo.

Kenyatta   *My* playground, *my* rules, George. Revolutionaries are allowed to let their hair down (*Beat. He pulls* **Pizer** *closer.*) Don't worry about your reputations here. The night knows how to keep secrets. (*Beat.*) My beloveds, this is your home away from home. Be free, be human. Get close, *real* close. Dancing is a mating ritual.

There's an immense excitement and an enjoyment of each other's bodies.

Kenyatta (*to* **Padmore**)   Come on, get up.

Padmore   Someone must be the responsible chaperone in the room.

Kenyatta   All work and no play, Georgie /

Padmore   Don't call me that. /

Kenyatta   This work can make men hard, and not in the fun way. Cut a rug my friend.

Pizer (*to* **Padmore**)   Let's show them how it's done.

Padmore   It's been a long day. I'm going to have another drink.

He turns away from them. The delegates exit, leaving **Nkrumah**, **Padmore**, **Ashwood Garvey**, **Kenyatta** *and* **Pizer** *on stage. The rest of Cosmopolitan exists off stage.*

Nkrumah (*to* **Appiah** *and* **Hlubi**)   I'll get us some drinks.

Padmore   Where's the whiskey, Jomo? /

Kenyatta *opens a locked shelf and hands* **Padmore** *a bottle of Eadie whiskey.* **Ashwood Garvey** *downs the last of her drink and slides her glass over to him.* **Padmore** *fills his and* **Ashwood Garvey**'s *glasses.*

Ashwood Garvey   Top me up too.

Nkrumah   A successful first day, George. Your Congress vision is alive.

Padmore *doesn't make eye contact with* **Nkrumah**. *He continues searching the bar.*

Padmore   It is not my vision alone. Abrahams is here. Banda is here. Milliard. Jomo, Amy /

Nkrumah   I didn't mean any disrespect. But it was your rallying call that brought us here. We should have written a catchy slogan and printed t-shirts with your glorious face on them.

Padmore   Showboating is unattractive, Nkrumah. /

Nkrumah   If your articles and pamphlets are anything to go by, the manifesto will be epic. I was thinking in the manifesto, we should have a section dedicated to the youth. They won't come to things like this. They need to be met on their terms, in their villages, on their street corners, (*Gestures to the room.*) in their bars. /

Padmore (*snaps*)   Kwame, let me enjoy my drink in silence.

Beat. The room stops. **Nkrumah** *feels everyone's eyes on him. He exits. Silence.*

Ashwood Garvey   Kwame is right. Today was fabulous.

Kenyatta   What's bothering you, George?

Padmore   We didn't hear from Du Bois or his people.

Pizer   Commercial flights are only just getting back up. He could still be on his way.

Padmore (*to* **Pizer**)   But what if it's something else? I've been careful not to overstep since the article.

Ashwood Garvey   What article?

Beat.

Padmore   I spoke to the Chicago Tribune during the trade unions conference in February. I was excited. We'd just had the largest Negro mass meeting in Manchester's history. I candidly mentioned that we should use the momentum to plan a Pan-African conference. The paper quoted me and he wrote to me soon after saying he was concerned that I was leaving the NAACP out. He was already planning a post-war congress. (*Beat.*) I suggested that we work together. But it's hard to inform him on everything, when decisions need to be made in the moment.

Ashwood Garvey   We don't need Du Bois's blessing for this week to be a success.

Padmore   The congresses are his brainchild.

Ashwood Garvey   Depending on who you ask. Ideas are rebranded and made popular by others all the time.

Padmore   He is influential. My reputation and credibility are on the line.

Ashwood Garvey   Americans arrogantly believe they're number one in the world in everything, including civil rights movements. You've done nothing wrong, George. Batons get passed on whether a predecessor is ready or not. (*Beat.*) Look around the room. There are Africans from all walks of life. Du Bois held four previous congresses and, in each one, he catered to the academic bourgeoisie. (*Beat.*) Du Bois simply doesn't like being outshined. You all remember how he saw Marcus and I as competition when the UNIA emerged. (*Beat.*) He called us a danger to our own people. Traitors. Meanwhile he was in the FBI's pocket. /

Kenyatta   Allegedly /

Ashwood Garvey   We reached the black masses whilst Du Bois was busy drinking tea with white friends and dancing at the Astoria. (*Beat.*) Jealousy made Du Bois write to you, George, nothing else.

Kenyatta   Give the man more respect, Amy. His writings on black America are groundbreaking. /

Ashwood Garvey   Jomo, this week is about all Africans, not just Americans.

Kenyatta *changes the subject.*

Kenyatta   The last time we were together like this, we'd been heckled and spat on at Speakers' Corner for being unpatriotic.

Padmore   I found all my pamphlets in the bin as we were leaving.

Ashwood Garvey (*refers to the audience and delegates off stage*) My parlour was our sanctuary just like the Cosmopolitan is theirs.

Pizer   Your curried goat is still the best seasoned food I've ever had.

Ashwood Garvey   Spam and Lord Woolton Pie are punishment. I couldn't let you suffer on the streets and in your stomachs too.

Kenyatta   I tried to teach Edna how to cook ugali and she turned it into a lumpy watery porridge. It made me miss my first wife.

Pizer   Jomo, you have another wife?

Kenyatta   Monogamy is a Western phenomenon.

Pizer   You're married to an English woman, Jomo.

Kenyatta   For anthropological purposes.

Pizer   So, loving us is a social experiment?

Kenyatta   My dear, loving anyone is a series of unknown variables.

They all cheers in agreement. **Appiah** *joins them.*

Appiah (*to* **Ashwood Garvey**)   Pardon me, Aunty. /

Ashwood Garvey   Excuse me?! Mi nuh yuh aunty! Mi still a young sexy uhman who cya ave yuh inna tailspin an lef yuh calling fi god inna di bedroom.

Kenyatta   Take a breath, Joseph. She's teasing you.

Appiah   I – I didn't mean any disrespect. I just wanted to say how much I admired your campaigning in New York. (*Beat.*) I'm a law student. Getting Adam Clayton Powell in the Unites States Congress is historic. I hope more black people become the first to conquer prominent positions.

Ashwood Garvey   I know what I have done. But what have you accomplished, Joseph?

Appiah   I am the current president of the West African Students' Union.

Ashwood Garvey   I helped Solanke set that up, you know.

Appiah   I told the boys that I would pay my respects to Iyalode, our founding mother. (*He kneels and gets back up.*) We have been doing you proud. The Nigerian Union of Students and the Sierra Leone Students' Union have affiliated now. Many of us want to go back home once our studies are finished. I'm here to make sure we voice our demands for independent states too.

Ashwood Garvey   Well, next time we meet, Joseph, I want to shake the hand of a country's president.

Appiah   I won't let you down.

Appiah *exits.*

Padmore (*to* **Pizer**)   I'm ready to call it a night.

Pizer   Me too.

Padmore   I'll get our coats.

Padmore *exits.*

Pizer   Thanks, love. (*Turns to* **Ashwood Garvey**.) He puts so much pressure on himself. He hasn't slept well in weeks.

Ashwood Garvey   Heavy is the head that wears the crown. (*Beat.*) Just keep being there.

Pizer   Wonderful work today, Chairman. Goodnight.

Pizer *exits.* **Dorman** *and* **Johnson** *approach the bar.*

Dorman   Another gin and tonic please, Jomo.

Johnson   I'll have a lemonade pop /

Ashwood Garvey *admires* **Johnson**.

Johnson (*to* **Ashwood Garvey**)   Good evening.

Beat.

Ashwood Garvey   It certainly is now.

Beat. He holds out his hand.

Johnson (*to* **Ashwood Garvey**)   Len.

Ashwood Garvey (*to* **Johnson**)   Amy.

Ashwood Garvey *keeps hold of his hand. She feels his muscles.* **La Badie** *enters.*

She straightens herself and approaches the bar.

Dorman (*to* **La Badie**)   Oi, you disappeared this morning. You can't be doing that.

La Badie *ignores her.*

La Badie   Excuse me, Mrs Ashwood Garvey, sorry to interrupt, I'm Alma /

Ashwood Garvey *gets up to hug her.*

Ashwood Garvey (*hugs her*)   Alma La Badie! I thought you'd not been able to make it.

La Badie   I was meant to arrive last night, but there was an incident at work.

Ashwood Garvey   I hope everything was alright?

La Badie   A baby was abandoned at the orphanage. A little girl.

Ashwood Garvey   How is she doing?

La Badie   We rushed her to the hospital, but she passed this morning.

Ashwood Garvey   Jesus.

Johnson   I'm sorry to hear that. (*Holds out his hand.*) Len. Len Johnson.

La Badie   Nice to meet you. (*To* **Ashwood Garvey**.) Pastor Ekarte was meant to drive me, but I told him to stay with the staff. They need his counsel. (*Beat.*) I thought I could make my own way this morning without getting lost, but I nearly missed my own talk.

Dorman (*to* **La Badie**)   You're a delegate? /

La Badie   Yes /

Dorman   Why didn't you say so? /

La Badie   Why didn't you ask me? /

Ashwood Garvey   You're the Secretary, Betty, you should know all the delegates /

Dorman   We have nearly 200 delegates representing fifty organisations from across the world. It's a lot of people to keep track of.

Ashwood Garvey   But Alma and I are the only women, *black* women speaking here, Betty. There's no excuses. (*To* **La Badie**.) I'm glad that you still came. (*Pulls out a chair for her.*) Come sit.

Nkrumah, **Appiah** *and* **Hlubi** *curiously approach with drinks in hand. They sit at table close by.* **Dorman** *feels like she's in the way. She joins the men at the table.* **Johnson** *remains at the bar. All eyes are on* **La Badie**.

La Badie   My mother has been telling me stories about you since I was little. I started to wonder if you were a myth.

Ashwood Garvey   I've heard plenty great things about you too. (*To* **Kenyatta**.) I don't get jealous of many people, Jomo, but this one is special. Even with all my friends in the Jamaican High Commission, I couldn't convince not one US government official to give work permits to the women and girls I was helping. Miss Alma La Badie slid right under my nose and secured her own permit to serve in the British Air Force. (*Beat.*) You are the shining role model for girls.

Johnson (*to* **La Badie**)   I heard your talk this morning. The plight of coloured babies in Britain hits very close to home.

La Badie (*to* **Johnson**)   Did you grow up in a home?

Johnson   No, but my mixed family stood out everywhere we went.

La Badie   I'm happy your parents stayed together. Are they [still in Manchester?] /

Kenyatta   The town hall is for discussions. The bar is for fun.

La Badie (*to* **Ashwood Garvey**)   Can I buy you a drink?

Ashwood Garvey *gets up to leave.*

Ashwood Garvey   If I drink more, I talk more, and George will complain that I'm not being a good role model. (*Beat.*) Are you speaking again?

La Badie   Yes, on Friday.

Ashwood Garvey   Wonderful. I'll be speaking tomorrow and on Friday. We should rehearse together.

La Badie   Really?

Ashwood Garvey   Wi black women haffi stick together, Alma. Find me tomorrow.

La Badie   Thank you.

Ashwood Garvey *exits.* **La Badie** *and* **Johnson** *remain at the bar.* **Kenyatta** *starts clearing up.*

La Badie (*to* **Johnson**)   Are you a speaker this week?

Johnson   No. I'm here observing for the Manchester Communist Party.

Dorman   Planning on getting into politics ?

They turn to face the table.

Johnson   I'm not a bureaucratic suit. I want to know the people I'm helping.

La Badie   As it should be. Men that go from one institution to another, end up disconnected to the real world.

Johnson   I see lot of African students on my route. They look like walking zombies coming off the campuses.

Nkrumah   You say African like as if you're not one of us.

Johnson   I'm a Manc, through and through.

Hlubi   But where are your people from?

Johnson   My father is Sierra Leonean, and my mam is Irish.

Appiah   Have you ever been to your homeland?

Johnson   Ireland or Sierra Leone?

Beat.

Nkrumah   You're an African. You should get to know yourself.

Johnson *notices the dig in* **Nkrumah***'s tone.*

Johnson   If I didn't know myself, I wouldn't have dominated so many of my opponents in the ring.

Hlubi   You box?

Dorman   Len's a Moss Side legend around here, Marko.

Johnson   I was pro for thirteen years until the colour bar ended that.

Hlubi   I've got a few moves myself.

Johnson *and* **Hlubi** *stand.* **Hlubi** *punches into his palms,*

Nkrumah   Stage fighting is not the same as real fighting, Marko. /

Nkrumah, **Dorman** *and* **Appiah** *laugh.* **La Badie** *is not as easily amused.*

Johnson   You're an actor? /

Hlubi   Yes /

Johnson   Man, that's a serious skill.

Hlubi   Finally, a friend who values my talent. You know I am a direct descendant of the great warrior King Shaka Zulu

Appiah (*coughs*)   Bullshit /

Hlubi   You're just jealous because your people aren't great warriors. /

Appiah   Come again?! /

Hlubi   You heard me! /

Nkrumah   We are a warrior nation!

Hlubi   But none of your warriors will ever be as famous as Shaka Zulu. When Hollywood makes a film about him, I will be ready for the casting call.

Nkrumah   We don't need Hollywood to make movies about our heroes to know we are great. /

Appiah   You Southern Africans always think you can compete with West Africans. /

Hlubi (*to* **Kenyatta**)   *Mzee*, Jomo, please jump in. We are supposed to be here for unity so why are we being subjected to this elitist xenophobia.

Kenyatta   West Africa is not the centre of the continent, boys. There are over 3,000 tribes in Africa. Respect us too. (*Beat.*) Your success in this life is determined by how you select, attract and retain mates. (*Beat.*) Study your community. Grasp what they need. *Harambee!* ('All pull together' in Kiswahili). Pull together. Tomorrow is a new day. Try again.

Kenyatta *turns off the bar sign. They all down their drinks.*

Congress Speech

A projection appears:

'DAY 2: 16 OCTOBER 1945'

Ashwood Garvey *and* **Pizer** *enter.* **Padmore** *steps to the mic holding a newspaper. The delegates surround him.*

Padmore   Congress, listen to the press's take on us (*To the audience.*) . . . News coming from England . . . The opening day at the Pan-African Congress was marred with bitterness . . . They claim the removal of British rule would immediately bring heaven to the colonies . . . the recklessness of speakers . . . Emotion rather than reason was the order of the day . . . The Special Branch should investigate the organisers . . . If their grievances are so intolerable, why don't they go home?

Nkrumah *interrupts* **Padmore** *by taking the mic.*

Nkrumah (*to the audience*)   Why don't *they* go home?! (*The room cheers.* **Padmore** *is forced to step aside.*) Imperialism is a parasite. Parasites are organisms that live on or in another organism, called the host. They get nutrients from it. Parasites can cause disease, pain or sometimes be almost unnoticeable to their host. (*Beat.*) Eradicating imperialism in Africa isn't just about removing the colonialist from positions of power. We must paralyse, kill and stop their growth of mutations on the continent, in our minds, in our cultures, in our children. (*Beat.*) Get out of *our* homelands. /

Appiah   *Firi ha ko!* ('Get out' in Twi.)

All   *Firi ha ko!*

Delegates repeats.

Nkrumah   Get out!

Hlubi   *Phumani!* ('Get out' in Zulu.)

All   *Phumani!*

Nkrumah   Get out!

Kenyatta   *Toka nje!* ('Get out' in Swahili.)

All   *Toka nje!*

Nkrumah   Get out !

Johnson   *Komot de!* ('Get out' in Krio.)

All   *Komot de!*

Delegates repeat the chants as they disperse. **Johnson** *and* **La Badie** *remain on stage.*

Scene Five

Black Man, Black Woman

Day 2: 16 October 1945, afternoon.

Boardroom, Chorlton-on-Medlock Town Hall.

La Badie   Di English boy ave a likkle seasoning.

Johnson (*to* **La Badie**)   My dad taught me a little Krio when I was a kid. It was our cheat code ring side.

La Badie   That's a good strategy.

Johnson   My old man was sharp like that. In training, he'd say, 'Boy, you go, go far!'

La Badie   He believed in you. My parents back home are just the same.

Johnson   They must be proud you're in England.

La Badie   Scared mostly. (*Beat.*) But when I put my mind to something, it's hard to make me stop.

Johnson   Even when we were being called sambo and my mam's face was getting slashed for being with my dad /

La Badie   What? /

Johnson   Yeah, yeah. My parents always told us, we were special. We were meant to be here.

La Badie   I've been wondering lately if I'm meant to be in England.

Johnson   You're doing good work.

La Badie   Maybe I'm just too far away from my people.

Johnson   You've found me and Amy here.

La Badie   Yes but, most people at this Congress have these big dreams. They want to rule countries and be in governments. They all understand each other. /

Johnson   They don't understand me. (*Beat.*) I'm not smart like them. I'm not black like them. But I'll never be white enough for England either. I've still got to figure out how to make this place liveable for my children. We're three generations deep now. It's our home, no matter what anyone says.

La Badie   I didn't even plan to make this country my home after the war. /

Johnson   You're a northern now, our kid. /

La Badie   It's all Pastor Ekarte's fault. I met him and ended up with a new dream here. (*Beat.*) I'm worried listening to the others is making my dream smaller.

Johnson   Then tell me before it disappears. (*She's hesitant.*) C'mon, Alma. I want to hear what you've got planned for our streets.

Beat.

La Badie   I wish I could find every abandoned child in time, and find a way to be there for all the ones in homes too. But there's only one of me. (*Beat.*) So, my dream is to chair a committee of distinguished negroes, starting in Liverpool, spreading to the rest of the world.

Johnson   A global network. I like it.

La Badie   People with money and connections who can offer internships for children when they age out of the welfare system.

Johnson   I can help you with that.

Beat.

La Badie   Do you have a magic wand, Mr Johnson?

Johnson (*laughs*)   No, but plenty influential people used to watch my fights. Paul Robeson is a friend. /

La Badie   You know Paul Robeson? /

Johnson   Don't tell, Marko. I'm scared he'll never leave me alone. /

La Badie   Who doesn't want to be friends with a Hollywood star. /

Johnson   He knows negroes in the arts, sports and politics. I can put you in touch.

Beat.

La Badie   Why would you do that?

Johnson   Every child should know the feeling of someone backing them like we did. (*Beat.*) Plus, my youngest is called Alma too. It'll be wrong if I don't help her namesake.

Beat.

La Badie   Thanks, Len. (*Beat.*) Listen, I've got rehearse before my practice with Amy.

Johnson   I'll find you later. We can put together a proposal to share with people.

La Badie   Okay, thanks.

He exits. Beat. **La Badie** *starts reciting her speech.*

La Badie (*recites*)   What the press will not tell you is that while officially there is no child labour in Jamaica, poverty makes it necessary for children to work alongside their parents on plantations. (*Beat.* **Nkrumah** *enters and lingers.*)

This is where the Union Jack flies high. (*Clears her throat. Repeats with more emphasis.*) This, is where, the Union Jack flies high.

Nkrumah   I prefer the second way. (**La Badie** *doesn't respond.*) Poverty and Child Labour in the Caribbean, 3 pm.

La Badie   So, you found me in the programme?

Nkrumah   I'm one of the rapporteurs. (*She nods and walks away. He calls out.*) We got off on the wrong foot yesterday.

She turns back.

La Badie   You and your little friend thought I was the help.

Nkrumah   Let's start again. (*Beat.*) I promise, I'm likable once you get to know me.

La Badie   Must I like you?

Nkrumah   Come on, Alma, I'm trying here.

Beat. He smiles.

La Badie   Does that cute smile usually work?

Nkrumah   You think I'm cute?

La Badie (*sucks her teeth and walks away*)   Boyish charms only work on girls.

Nkrumah   That's why I like grown women.

La Badie   Jesus wept.

La Badie *turns to leave.*

Nkrumah   I saw Amy go downstairs.

La Badie *turns back.* **Nkrumah** *blocks her path. She steps aside. He mirrors her.*

La Badie   Is Betty not here to play with you today?

Nkrumah   She is helping the Entertainment Committee.

La Badie   So, you're wasting my time instead?

Beat. She steps aside. He mirrors her. Beat.

Nkrumah   You and Betty can be friends too you know.

La Badie   If Betty wants to be my friend, she can talk to me herself.

Nkrumah   Will she get the same frosty reception? (**La Badie** *scoffs and walks on.*) She's a sweet girl. She's committed to the movement.

La Badie   She types a few documents so now she understands our struggles?

Nkrumah   Criticism alone doesn't teach anyone, Alma.

La Badie (*turns back*)   Who said I want to teach Betty anything?

Beat.

Nkrumah   Not all white people are evil.

La Badie   Do you say that about the white men too, or just the white women who find you attractive?

Beat.

Nkrumah   I see clearly not all black people were raised right /

La Badie   You don't know anything about how I was raised. /

Nkrumah   And you don't know anything about me, yet you keep passing judgements on me. I've been through struggles you'll never know. /

La Badie   We all have struggles, you're not that special. /

Nkrumah   I'm not competing with you, Alma. /

La Badie   How about we stop talking to each other for the rest of the week? /

She walks away.

Nkrumah (*calls out*)   This week is about solidarity.

La Badie   Solidarity doesn't mean I must be in community with everyone.

Nkrumah   You'll never win with that mentality. (**La Badie** *stops.*) I can help you with whatever cause you have. I'm connected too. I know who George knows.

Pause. **La Badie** *approaches him.*

La Badie   Then it sounds like I should be going directly to George, not the mentee hanging on his coat tails.

Pause. She walks away.

Nkrumah   Be careful you don't become Amy. She's burnt many bridges mocking Marcus in her musicals. In these circles, networks are everything.

Beat. **La Badie** *turns back.* **Ashwood Garvey** *enters and lingers. They don't notice her.*

La Badie   I'd proudly be Amy, over the fraud that Marcus was. /

Nkrumah   Marcus's words were manna from heaven. Four million Garveyites globally believed in *him*. *He* sold out Madison Square Garden. What activist do you know that can do that today? /

La Badie   No man should ever be above the movement. /

Nkrumah   Movements need confident leaders. /

La Badie   Leaders built on edited history and complicit followers are not what we need.

Beat.

Nkrumah   We have plenty threats against us out there, we don't need one in here. /

La Badie   I'm not the threat /

Nkrumah   We need everyone's support, especially black women. /

La Badie   Do you want my support or obedience, Kwame?

Beat.

Nkrumah   Mobilising the black man is mobilising the black woman.

Beat. She steps closer to him.

La Badie   Then stand behind me. (*Beat.*) Let me lead you, (*Beat.*) or can't you handle that?

Pause. **Ashwood Garvey** *steps forward.*

Ashwood Garvey (*to* **La Badie**)   That's enough, Alma, your mind is not a sample for these men to try. We've got work to do. (*To* **Nkrumah**.) Go run errands for George. (*To* **La Badie**.) Come.

Ashwood Garvey *and* **La Badie** *exit.* **Nkrumah** *is alone on stage.*

Dorman *enters. She's wiping flour off her clothes.*

Dorman   Kwame, I've been looking for you. I need to pop back home to get changed. My dress got mucky. Ras had me making dumplings for Guyanese *metamgee*. Is that even how you say it? Can you take my notes for George this afternoon? /

Nkrumah   Am I a joke here or something? Do people not see how much I am doing. I'm not incompetent because I'm George's mentee. /

Dorman   What's been said? (*He paces. She approaches him.*) Talk to me.

Pause.

Nkrumah   I almost became a Jesuit priest, you know.

Beat.

Dorman   I can't imagine you in a robe.

Beat.

Nkrumah   When I was baptised as a boy, the Catholics told our parents in the village that God's hand in our lives would be like beams of sunlight touching the darkest depths of our oceans. (*Beat.*) But as I got older and migrated to study, I saw that the world didn't treat me like I was made in His image.

Dorman   What are you saying, Kwame?

Beat.

Nkrumah   I've spent so many years conflicted about who I was. CLR told me to leave New York and come meet George Padmore. George turns dreams into a reality, he said. (*Beat.*) I thought coming here would be another rebirth, but even this is seeming like a con. (*Beat.*) I won't waste any more time being groomed into obedience. (*Beat.*) I've been away from home for a decade. If I'm going to liberate my people, I need my name on that manifesto. It will give context to who I am, what I've been doing and to legitimize my purpose back home. (*Beat.*) George is holding back the key to my progress.

Beat.

Dorman   So, let's take the keys.

Nkrumah   How?

Beat.

Dorman   Dorothy holds the keys, George. (*Beat.*) She's the only person I've ever seen him listen to without arguing. (*Beat.*) You charmed half of those biddies when we were out canvassing. (*Beat.*) You can handle Dorothy.

Beat. He steps closer to her.

Nkrumah (*smiles to* **Dorman**)   You always make me feel better.

Beat. She radiates. **Dorman** *kisses him.* **Pizer** *enters and catches them. They pull away from each other.*

Pizer   Kwame, don't you have a session to be in. (*Beat.* **Nkrumah** *exits.* **Dorman** *turns to leave.*) Betty, stay.

Dorman *turns back.* **Pizer** *approaches her.*

Pizer   I chose you to work here because you came highly recommended from secretarial college.

Dorman   Haven't I been doing good work?

Beat.

Pizer   What are you doing with Kwame?

Dorman   We like each other.

Pizer   Betty, Kwame has big dreams. /

Dorman   I know. /

Pizer   No, you don't /

Dorman   Yes, I do. We talk all the time. (*Beat.*) I know him. (*Beat.*) I'm helping him like the way you help George. /

Pizer   Don't compare yourselves to us /

Dorman   Why not? /

Pizer   Because it's more than kissing and typing manuscripts /

Dorman   Is it because he's a negro? (*Beat.*) My dad's been asking me to work somewhere else. But I told him the Federation does good work for the trade unions, just like he does /

Pizer   And what did he say about the Congress and Africa? (*Pause.*) You can't repeat that can you. (*Beat.*) Focus on your work and nothing else.

Hlubi *enters.*

Hlubi   Secretary Betty, tell me, are the rumours about George true? /

Pizer   What rumours? /

Hlubi (*surprised*)   Yoh. (*Beat.*) Hi, Dorothy. /

Pizer   What rumours, Marko? /

Hlubi   George and Du Bois have fallen out, that's why he's not coming. /

Dorman   George doesn't tell me everything. /

Pizer   He tells me everything. (*Beat.*) There's no rift. Stop spreading lies.

Pizer *exits.*

Congress Speech

The delegates flood the stage. All eyes on **Padmore**. **Pizer** *is protective of him.*

A projection:

'DAY 3: 17 OCTOBER 1945'

Kenyatta *steps to a mic.*

Kenyatta (*to the audience*)   Many of us talk about home, but have no home, because to have a home, you must have a land on which you stand your house or hut and say, 'This is my home'. From Somaliland to Kenya, Uganda, Tanganyika and Nyasaland; no African can claim that right. (*To the audience.*) Home is identity. But who are? (*Beat.*) Our kings answer to the assistant of the District Commissioner. We harvest our coffee on white plantations. Our names are no longer songs our ancestors sang freely. They're caged in little boxes around our necks for the police to check. (*Beat.*) Our identities have been systemically eroded for generations. Independence will give us the right of citizenship and to be who we are.

The delegates disperse. **Nkrumah** *approaches* **Pizer**.

Scene Six

Tactics

Day 3: 17 October 1945, afternoon.

Upstairs corridor, Chorlton-on-Medlock Town Hall.

Nkrumah   Dorothy, can I grab you quickly?

Pizer   Not now. I don't want to miss the start of Ras's speech /

Nkrumah   What you saw yesterday, between me and Betty. It was nothing. We are just friends.

Pizer   Does she know that? (*Beat.*) Love and activism both require a lot of attention, Kwame. George needs your focus here. /

Nkrumah   And he has it. I've learnt a lot from him, from you both. I hope you see that.

Pizer   Keep doing your work /

She turns to leave.

Nkrumah   I want to take on more responsibility.

She turns back.

Pizer   Your work on the committee isn't finished.

Nkrumah   George keeps saying we have a short window to start building nations and he wants to put down some scaffolding. I can help him do that /

Pizer   George doesn't want to be a statesman. /

Nkrumah   But I do. (*Beat.*) He said we'd talk about my involvement in the manifesto. But it's been three days, I've barely spoken to him. Can you remind him of this?

Beat.

Pizer   George gets tunnel vision when he has any project on. The Congress is the scale of a hundred big projects.

Nkrumah   CLR also sent me to him as a project too. (*Beat.*) Has he forgotten that?

Pizer   George honours his commitments.

Nkrumah   Or does he think he's done all that he can with me?

Pizer   Why would you say that?

Beat.

Nkrumah   I found some letters in George's office.

Beat.

Pizer   What letters?

Beat.

Nkrumah   The ones CLR wrote about me.

Pizer   You were snooping in George's things?

Nkrumah   He'd asked me to fetch some papers last week.

Pizer   Those letters were not meant for you to read.

Nkrumah   They were mocking me.

Pizer   You misread.

Nkrumah   It was right there in black and white,

'This young man is coming to you. He is not very bright George, but nevertheless do what you can for him because he's determined to throw Europeans out of Africa.' (*Beat.*) Do what he *can*? (*Beat.*)He made me sound like an idealistic lost cause. George had an assumption about me long before I arrived. /

Pizer   George can make up his own mind.

Nkrumah   I didn't come here a novice, Dorothy. I've published on Europeans governments in Africa and education. I've organised student activists. I have degrees upon degrees. /

Pizer   You're not the first mentee we've had with experience, Kwame. George is treating you the same as all the others before /

Nkrumah   I'm sorry, Dorothy, but that's a lie! (*Beat.*) I've been in your home. /

Pizer   As have others! /

Nkrumah   Yes, but after we've debated politics, planned the Congress, broken bread and drank bottles of wine, the others went home. You go to bed, and then it's me and George, sat at your kitchen table with his hands in the nooks and crannies of my soul. (*Beat.*) He shares private things with me. (*Beat.*) Things that trouble him.

Beat.

Pizer   Things like what? (*Beat.* **Nkrumah** *is reluctant to share*.) Oh no, you don't get to ask for my help and then go silent when I have questions.

Pause.

Nkrumah   He's mentioned Blyden and Julia a few times.

Beat.

Pizer   What about them?

Beat.

Nkrumah   He feels like he abandoned them.

Beat.

Pizer   He said that?

Beat.

Nkrumah   When they finally joined him in New York, he wasn't the father and husband they'd known back in Trinidad. (*Beat.*) Malcolm, the medical student was now renamed George, a radical activist with ambitions beyond providing for a family.

Beat.

Pizer   People change.

Nkrumah   But at what cost? (*Beat.*) After twenty years of activism, every telephone is tapped. He gets death threats. He walks these streets not knowing a passer-by from an assassin.

Pizer   It's the sacrifice we all live with in this work.

Nkrumah   He lost his wife and child, Dorothy.

Beat.

Pizer   George and Julia's marriage ended for many reasons.

Beat.

Nkrumah   He wants his life to mean something. (*Beat.*) He needs to have someone carrying the load, carrying his vision forward. (*Beat.*) George and I are very similar. (*Beat.*) Changing our names was a rite of passage towards our legacy. (*Beat.*) Talk to him, for me.

Beat. **Pizer** *is ruminating on* **Nkrumah***'s words. Beat. She steps closer to him.*

Pizer   Kwame.

Nkrumah (*smiles*)   Yes?

Beat.

Pizer   You are very ambitious. (*Beat.*) But if you want something from George, don't use me. Have the balls to be a man and talk to him yourself.

The delegates flood the stage. **Padmore** *and* **Nkrumah** *find each other in the crowd. Face to face. They size each other up.*

Congress Speech

Hlubi *steps to the mic.*

Hlubi   The African is frustrated.

Appiah, **Johnson** *and* **Kenyatta** *notice the tension.*

Hlubi   In South Africa, the Riotous Assembly Act prevents us meting to voice protests.

Pizer *is distant from* **Padmore**. **Dorman** *shadows* **Nkrumah**.

Hlubi   It is a crime for me to address you. This is a prohibited meeting by law.

Ashwood Garvey *and* **La Badie** *keep to themselves at a distance.*

Hlubi   To do so, we are deemed threats to public peace. Penalties include fines and imprisonment. (*Beat.*) However, the white unions regularly meet. (*Beat.*) They exclude us from their meetings. (*Beat.*) The industrial development sent us en-masse into the cities looking for work. (*Beat.*) But they herded us into allocations – ghettos. Our homes are shanties made from rubbish. Overcrowding is a nightmare. Diseases are rampant. The death toll is high. We have no health insurance. No pensions. Low wages and criminal charges if you're late to the mines. (*Beat.*) The African is frustrated. (*Beat.*) But we're forbidden to say it out loud.

Pizer *rushes out quickly. The room is about to clear when* **Nkrumah** *addresses the room. They all stop and watch them.*

Scene Seven

Respectability Politics

Day 3: 17 October 1945, late afternoon.

Upstairs Gallery, Chorlton-on-Medlock Town Hall.

Nkrumah (*to the room*)   I'm putting out a new press release tomorrow morning to address the rumours that have been circulating.

Padmore   No you're not.

Padmore *turns to leave.*

Nkrumah   I'm Joint Secretary too, George.

He turns back.

Padmore (*to the room*)   If delegates have time to gossip over dead cups of tea, (*To* **Nkrumah**.) then you're not focusing on why we're here.

Kenyatta (*to the room*)   I heard the volunteers baked cakes at the restaurant. Get a slice before it's all gone.

The room starts to disperse again but are stopped when **Nkrumah** *speaks up.*

Nkrumah   The Padmore that CLR told me about was militant. He would jump to correct rumours that question his character. (*Beat.*) But the longer I'm here, I see your flame is a dimming spark. /

Kenyatta   Watch yourself, boy. My friend has earned his respect. /

Nkrumah (*to* **Padmore**)   You risked your life to smuggle Communist pamphlets and now, you're more concerned about respectability?

Padmore   Am I disappointment to you?

Nkrumah   A teacher should want his student to surpass him. But every time, I've asked to co-write the manifesto, /

Padmore   Not this again /

Nkrumah   You keep brushing me off. /

Appiah   Have you earned it? /

Nkrumah   He's worse than my supervisor Joe. /

Appiah   George has given you plenty of his time. /

Nkrumah (*to* **Appiah**)   I came to him /

Padmore   I didn't ask you to do that. There were plenty mentors in New York. /

Nkrumah   I'm done with mentors. I have ideas that could write manifestos. /

Padmore (*laughs*)   Manifestos about what?

Beat. **Nkrumah** *searches for a title.*

Nkrumah   Nkrumaism.

The room scoffs and laughs.

Kenyatta   And what will be your political strategy? /

Padmore   Vanity /

Nkrumah   A new Africa. /

Kenyatta   The old Africa still has traditions that can save us. /

Nkrumah   Science and technology will drive the youth into the future. /

Padmore   They need clear plans, not utopian pipe dreams /

Nkrumah   They need a borderless African super state, free from colonial rule and under one government /

La Badie   So, authoritarianism is your vision? /

Padmore (*to* **La Badie**)   He's more grandiloquence than pragmatism, Miss Alma /

Nkrumah   And he acts like all he does is set up these platforms for us to organise, (*To* **Padmore**.) but you are the puppeteer /

Padmore   I'm not in control of anything.

Kenyatta   *We* have a committee. *We* selected delegates who are in sessions right now, and that is where you should be, opening your ears /

Padmore (*to* **Kenyatta**)   Learning strategic solution.

Nkrumah   Personality is my solution. /

Appiah   The cult of personality will be a distraction for our people, Kwame /

Padmore   If idolatry was a sustainable liberation tactic, we'd all have been freed during the Garveys' ostentatious parades through Harlem. /

Ashwood Garvey *clocks the dig at her.*

Hlubi   The fall from revolutionary to pariah can be very fast if you're not careful. /

Nkrumah (*to* **Hlubi**)   Especially if you have disloyal comrades, (*Turns to* **Padmore**.) publishing premature obituaries killing you before your time. /

Padmore   That was a miscommunication of the facts. I apologised to Marcus. /

Nkrumah   You won't ruin my legacy too. /

Hlubi (*pulling* **Nkrumah** *back*)   Don't speak to George like that. /

Nkrumah   Wake up, Marko, he's not above criticism. /

Appiah   But how you give it matters too /

Dorman *touches his arm. He shrugs her off.*

Dorman   Kwame, let's go for a walk /

Nkrumah   I don't want to bloody walk with you. /

Dorman *is taken aback.* **Johnson** *steps to him and points his hand in his face.* **Nkrumah** *smacks it away.*

Johnson   Don't talk to her like that! /

Johnson *clenches his fists but restrains himself.*

Padmore   Me, me, me, me. Nothing about we, that is why you're not editing the Congress manifesto.

Nkrumah   Fine. (*Beat.*) I'll write my own manifesto. (*Turns to everyone.*) You are welcome to read it and compare /

Padmore *steps to* **Nkrumah**.

Padmore   You're playing a dangerous game, Nkrumah.

Nkrumah *steps closer to* **Padmore**.

Nkrumah   Are you afraid of a challenger, George?

Padmore *closes the gap.*

Padmore   If you don't like how I am doing things here, you are welcome to leave.

Pizer *rushes in.*

Pizer   George /

Padmore (*snaps at her*) What?!

Beat. **Pizer** *holds her gaze on* **Padmore**. *Her patience is wearing thin with him.*

Pizer   Du Bois is here. He didn't get your telegram moving the Congress to Manchester. They've been going around London looking for us.

Padmore *breathes a sigh of relief. The room remains tense. He adjusts his tie and regains his posture. Beat.*

Padmore (*smiles to the room*)   Right everyone, our guest of honour has arrived! (*Beat.*) Best faces forward. (*Beat.*) Dorothy, put him in the boardroom. Betty, in the top drawer of my office there's a gift for Mr Du Bois. Get it. (**Dorman** *exits. Beat.*) Len, when word gets out, they'll mob him. Help with crowd control. (**Len** *nods.*) Amy,

Ashwood Garvey   Yes.

Padmore   It would be a personal favour to me, and everyone else if you'd let Du Bois to step in as Congress chair.

Beat.

Ashwood Garvey   For the rest of the day?

Padmore   For the rest of the Congress.

Ashwood Garvey *looks around the room. Everyone is pleased. She makes eye contact with* **La Badie**. *Her expression is displeased.* **Ashwood Garvey** *smiles politely. Beat.*

Ashwood Garvey   Sure.

Beat.

Padmore   Excellent! (*Beat. To* **Hlubi**.) Marko, tomorrow morning, I want an impressive start. /

Ashwood Garvey *steps aside and lights a cigarette.*

Hlubi   Yes, boss! (*To the room.*) Everyone, for my second speech I'm going to try something different, a performance.

Padmore   This is it, everyone. Let's go!

Padmore *and* **Kenyatta** *excitedly exit.* **Pizer** *trails behind them.* **Appiah**, **Hlubi** *and* **Johnson** *are angry with* **Nkrumah**. *They exit as a new group.* **Nkrumah** *feels the scornful looks from* **La Badie**. *He exits. Silence.* **Ashwood Garvey** *is pacing and quietly seething. She doesn't make eye contact with* **La Badie**.

La Badie   Suh dis a wah happens at dem yah tings? Di boys club more like a girl's boarding school and everyone menstruating. (*Beat.* **Ashwood Garvey** *doesn't respond.*) George surprised you with his announcement, didn't he? (*Beat.*) I'm sorry, Amy, you've been doing a fine job /

Ashwood Garvey (*snaps*)   Oh, I know I do a fine job! I don't need you to pity me. They can have Du Bois. It's not a step down for me. (*Beat.*) Let this be a lesson to you, Alma. They will never see you. They will never respect you. The first chance these men get, they will sacrifice you to make false gods of themselves. (*Beat.*) Now if you're not strong enough to handle that, then *likkle* girl, you'll never be as great as me.

She flicks her cigarette and exits. Beat. **La Badie** *fights back her tears. She exits.*

Act Two

Scene One

The Gloves Are Off

Day 4 : 18 October 1945, evening.

Cosmopolitan Club.

Kenyatta *turns on the 'COSMOPOLITAN' sign above the bar. A projection:*

'Day 4: 18 October 1945'

Padmore, Johnson, Dorman, Appiah *and* **Hlubi** *(adorned with a Zulu headring, ceremonial belts and ankle rattles) are on the dance floor.* **La Badie** *sits alone.* **Nkrumah, Pizer** *and* **Ashwood Garvey** *make their way to the bar.* **Dorman** *looks over at* **Nkrumah,** *attempting to make him jealous.* **Johnson** *gestures over to* **La Badie** *to join them. She refuses and remains at a table.*

Padmore *does a little two step.* **Johnson, Appiah, Hlubi** *and* **Dorman** *cheer him on.* **Ashwood Garvey** *nudges* **Pizer** *to look. She glances over and turns back around to the bar.*

Kenyatta *studies the segregated room.* **Ashwood Garvey, Nkrumah** *and* **Pizer** *are spread along the bar.* **Pizer** *nurses a sherry. Her energy is lower than usual.* **Ashwood Garvey** *leans over the bar and steals a bottle of whiskey. She's nearing a drunk state. She overfills her glass.* **Kenyatta** *wrestles the bottle from her.* **Nkrumah** *writes in his notebook.* **Hlubi** *ululates and whistles loudly. He circles* **Padmore, Dorman, Appiah, La Badie** *and* **Johnson**.

Hlubi *(to the audience)*   For those that missed my sold-out performance this morning /

Appiah   It wasn't ticketed.

Hlubi *(to* **Appiah***)   Voetsek!* ('Go away' in Afrikaans.) I decided to perform a call to the ancestors to rebalance the energies here. I will perform an encore at the Cosmopolitan. I need Zulu warriors. (*To* **Padmore**, **Appiah**, **Dorman** *and* **Johnson**.) Please get into formation and copy me. Alma, that includes you too. Come, come. (*They all get into a line. He whistles and kicks high in the Zulu ingoma dance style.*) Now you try. /

Padmore (*laughs*)   My hips won't allow it, Marko! /

Dorman   Everyone will see my knickers. /

Hlubi   Fine. (*To the audience.*) But when I point to you, I want you to say, '*Ubuntu*'. It means humanity, I am because we are.

He ululates, whistles again and kicks high. He points.

Padmore/Dorman/Appiah/La Badie/Johnson (*disorderly*) Ubuntu.

He shakes his head in disappointment.

Hlubi (*speaks*)   *Hayi hayi madoda* ('No, no, my guys'). Dancing is a holy act to Africans. Your ancestors deserve much more energy, more reverence, more rhythm. /

Dorman   My ancestors are Mancunian. /

Hlubi   Find rhythm from somewhere, Betty. (*To the audience.*) Now, remember when I point, *everyone* joins in.

He ululates, whistles again and kicks high. He points to the audience.

All   *Ubuntu*

Hlubi   *Yimina*. ('Me'.)

Points to the audience.

All   *Ubuntu*

Hlubi   *Nguwe*. ('You'.)

Uma ungithanda, uzithanda wena (If you love me, you love yourself)

Uma ungizwisa ubuhlungu, uzilimaza wena (If you hurt me, you hurt yourself)

Uma ungivikela, uyazivikela (If you protect me, you protect yourself.)

Ngoba (Because.)

Points to the audience.

All   *Ubuntu*

Hlubi   *Yimina.*

Points to the audience.

All   *Ubuntu* (Humanity is.)

Hlubi   *Nguwe* (You.)

Points to the audience.

All   (*Ubuntu.*)

He ululates.

Hlubi   We are one.

He takes a bow. **Padmore Dorman**, **La Badie**, **Johnson**, **Hlubi** *and* **Appiah** *applaud themselves.* **Pizer**, **Nkrumah** *and* **Ashwood Garvey** *don't join in.* **Kenyatta** *is not impressed by their lack of enjoyment.*

Kenyatta   You guys are killing the vibe.

Ashwood Garvey   Give me back the bottle and I'll have whatever vibe you want.

Kenyatta   You're cut off. (**Ashwood Garvey** *takes out a flask from her bra and drinks. To* **Pizer**.) Dorothy, this isn't like you.

Pizer   I think the adrenaline rush is finally wearing off.

Ashwood Garvey   Looks like George has found his second wind though.

Padmore *is holding court with* **Dorman**, **Johnson**, **La Badie**, **Hlubi** *and* **Appiah**. **Hlubi** *rests his head on* **Dorman**'s *shoulder. She strokes his hair whilst looking over at* **Nkrumah**. **Dorman** *notices* **La Badie** *watching her disapprovingly.* **Appiah** *and* **Hlubi** *call* **Nkrumah** *over. He turns his back on them.*

Padmore   I hope you all introduced yourselves to Du Bois.

Hlubi   Is he coming for a drink after his press interviews? /

Padmore   As great as he is, even he bows to old age. I'm taking him back to his accommodation to rest soon.

Appiah   He signed my copy Dusk of Dawn. I'm going to buy copies of his other books at Ras's store before we leave and get him to sign them too.

Hlubi   He said he will introduce me to Hollywood producers.

Johnson   He said I should stand as Moss Side MP and fight the colour bar from the inside.

Dorman   Everybody knows you. You'd easily win.

Padmore   Ask him to write you an endorsement letter.

Johnson   D'you think he'd do it? He doesn't lend his name to anyone.

Appiah   If you become a member of parliament, you won't be just anyone then.

Dorman   If you're aiming that high, speak to Ras. He's got Labour connections.

Padmore   If it wasn't for him, we wouldn't have had a venue for this week, accommodation for the delegates, or restaurants to eat at.

Dorman   Dream big, Len! I could be your campaign manager. I canvassed a lot for the Congress. George can vouch for my references.

Padmore   Len and Betty, changing Manchester together.

Dorman   Sounds pretty good.

Padmore   Miss Alma, what have you got to share?

Johnson (*to* **Padmore**)   We talked about a proposal. /

La Badie (*to* **Johnson**)   It's not ready to share. /

Padmore (*to* **La Badie**)   Write it quickly and give it to Du Bois. /

La Badie   Maybe /

Hlubi (*to* **Dorman**)   Your hair smells so good. (*Beat.*) Is that lavender?

Appiah *pulls him away.*

Appiah   Alright lover boy, leave Betty alone.

Dorman *pulls him back.*

Dorman   Oh, I don't mind taking care of my boys.

Hlubi *nestles in. The men laugh.* **La Badie** *doesn't laugh.* **Padmore***'s joy feels like a betrayal to* **Pizer**, **Ashwood Garvey** *and* **Nkrumah**.

Padmore   Right, I'm going to meet Du Bois. Keep planning great things. Goodnight.

Johnson (*to the table*)   Another round?

They all agree. **Johnson** *gestures for* **La Badie***'s help.*

Padmore (*goes to the bar*)   Jomo, make sure Dorothy gets home safely.

Kenyatta   Of course.

Padmore (*kisses her on the cheek*)   See you at home.

She doesn't respond. He exchanges looks with **Nkrumah** *as he exits.*

Johnson (*to* **Kenyatta**)   An orangeade pop, two beers, a G and T, water for Marko and a cola for Alma.

La Badie   No, a rum please, Jomo.

Johnson (*pats* **Nkrumah** *on the back hard*)   The days I fought with my coach, I lost in the ring. (**Nkrumah** *doesn't reply.*) Only the greats are disciplined, mate.

Nkrumah   But you quit when the colour bar made it harder /

Johnson   You don't know how hard I fought against them. They ruined me. They ruined the sport for me.

Nkrumah   Independence isn't a sport. It's life or death. (*Beat.*) The committed never quit.

Beat.

Johnson   I've met cleverer baiters than you, mate.

Beat. **Nkrumah** *stands.*

Nkrumah   I am not your bloody mate /

Ashwood Garvey *pulls* **Johnson** *away from* **Nkrumah**.

Ashwood Garvey   Now that I've got some free time, I want to see the sights of Manchester.

Nkrumah *moves to another table.* **Appiah**, **Hlubi** *and* **Dorman** *watch him across the room.*

Johnson   I know the city like the back of my hands.

She takes his hands into hers.

Ashwood Garvey   I know something else your hands can get to know better.

Johnson *laughs.*

La Badie   He's married. /

Ashwood Garvey   We're all married, Alma /

Kenyatta   Run, boy, run.

La Badie *is embarrassed for* **Ashwood Garvey**. **Johnson** *and* **La Badie** *return to the table with the drinks.*

Kenyatta (*to* **Ashwood Garvey**)   Is this the kind of role model you wanted to be?

Ashwood Garvey   I'll do it my way and George can do it his way.

She downs her drink.

Pizer   He didn't tell me that he was going to ask you to step down, Amy.

Kenyatta   Maybe he was excited and did it in the moment.

Ashwood Garvey   He had time to wrap a gift. What did I get, Jomo? (*Beat.*) Introduced as Marcus's ex-wife.

Kenyatta *pours them drinks.*

Kenyatta   To be fair to George, how are we supposed to know when to unlink your histories with Marcus. You contested your divorce decree for over twenty years.

Ashwood Garvey   No one diminishes your accomplishments when you talk about your multiple wives. (*Beat.*) Let Marcus rest in Kensal Green.

Kenyatta   Wasn't he repatriated back to Jamaica?

Ashwood Garvey   I had him entombed.

Kenyatta   At Amy's behest?

Ashwood Garvey   Yes, at my orders /

Kenyatta   You know who I mean. The other Amy. His wife. Amy, the mother of his children.

La Badie *keeps an eye on* **Ashwood Garvey**. *She can hear her getting louder.* **Dorman**'s *behaviour with the men also annoys her.* **Dorman** *notices her glares.*

Ashwood Garvey   There's too much base inna yuh voice. Reduce it. (*Beat.*) I'm still his legal wife. She's the cheap copy of me.

Kenyatta   Amy, it's not right to interrupt a transitioning spirit. *Ndukagerekanie gikuu na toro* /

Ashwood Garvey   I don't want to hear any more of your proverbs. /

Kenyatta   I will still say it, don't compare death with sleep.

Ashwood Garvey   He'll go back when everyone sees me as a national hero too. /

Kenyatta   He needs to rest in his ancestral land, not a foreign tomb. /

Ashwood Garvey   If Jamaica wants to bury their hero, they'll have to admit that I'm not the infidel and thief who ruined the UNIA. I wasn't innocent, but he was cruel too.

Kenyatta   When love turns bitter /

Pizer   No, Jomo, you don't get to question her behaviour. We know what he was like behind the work.

Ashwood Garvey   *He* married my maid of honour, my best friend. *He* hired thugs to break into my home. To strip me of furniture and clothes. *He* bedded plenty plenty white women across Europe whilst I worked to the bone to build our name back home. (*Beat.*) His love tasted bitter long before I wore the scarlet letter.

Beat. **Kenyatta** *accepts defeat. He pours the women more drinks.*

Johnson (*to* **La Badie**)   You've been quiet today.

La Badie   Just taking the week in.

Johnson   I hope I didn't overstep mentioning the proposal. /

La Badie   It's fine.

Johnson (*to* **Appiah**)   So why didn't Kwame leave?

Hlubi   Maybe he's cooled off. We should talk to him, Joe.

Appiah   I'm not chasing after him. /

Johnson   I can talk to him again. /

Hlubi   No! We are his friends. (*He stands.* **Appiah** *and* **Dorman** *remain seated.*) Joe? Betty?

Appiah   He's dogmatic.

Dorman   You saw how he spoke to me. I'm staying right here.

Hlubi *sucks his teeth and approaches* **Nkrumah**. **Nkrumah** *continues writing and doesn't address him. The room watches them.*

Hlubi   So, you were never co-writing with George. You didn't have to lie to us.

Nkrumah   He has no reason to say no. He laughs away my ideas to stay relevant. But we can all construct our own methods of liberation. After the Congress, we can form our own inner circles. We are the future Marko. /

Hlubi   We're already in a circle. (*Refers to the notebook.*) And your so-called manifesto is premature. Give it time /

Nkrumah   I'm not you, Marko! I'm not going to be a dog for the rest of my life, begging Hollywood for crumbs.

Hlubi   I don't have to justify myself to you /

Nkrumah   You settle when you could be telling your own stories. At this rate, you'll never be remembered as someone that mattered in history /

Appiah *shouts in defence from across the room.*

Appiah   Take that back, Kwame!

Appiah *approaches them.*

Hlubi   You know the difference between me and you, Kwame, is that I'm not chasing some elusive idea of myself. I already know I matter now.

Hlubi *sucks his teeth and exits.*

Dorman   Marko, don't go.

Appiah (*to* **Nkrumah**)   What's wrong with you? Marko is the only one that cared enough to speak to you.

Nkrumah   I want better for him /

Appiah   You don't get to dictate that for him. He gets to make choices about his art. But once your so-called manifesto is written into law what choices will our people have if they disagree with you? (*Beat.*) *Nyansapo wosane no badwemma.* (*Beat.*) The knot of wisdom is untied by the wise child. That is your tribe's proverb. You've forgotten that and it's why you're sitting in exile. Do you want this to be your legacy back home too? (**Nkrumah** *doesn't respond.* **Appiah** *sucks his teeth and leaves.*) Goodnight, everyone.

At the bar.

Ashwood Garvey   Pssst! Jomo. (*Takes out the 'CHAIRMAN' sign from her bra and places it on the bar. Beat.*) Look what I have.

Pizer   George has been looking for that. /

Ashwood Garvey   It's mine!

Kenyatta *tries to snatch it.* **Ashwood Garvey** *shoves it back inside her bra. They all laugh.* **La Badie** *returns to the bar.*

La Badie   Another rum, please, Jomo.

Ashwood Garvey   Me too. (*Beat.*) I'm going to the lavatory.

As she leaves, she stumbles, **La Badie** *rushes to catch her.*

La Badie   Maybe you've had enough, Amy /

Ashwood Garvey *snatches her arm away.*

Ashwood Garvey   Get off me! I can mind my damn self.

Ashwood Garvey *exits.*

Pizer   She doesn't mean to be cruel, Alma.

La Badie   It hurts like she does.

La Badie *gets a drink and sits at the end of the bar alone.*
Dorman *approaches* **Nkrumah**.

Dorman   Was this your plan all along? To lose all your friends this week.

Nkrumah   Betty, I already have a lot on my mind. /

Dorman   Since when do you speak to me like that? (*Beat.*) Look me in the eyes, Kwame. (*He looks up at her. Beat.*) I don't even recognise you.

Nkrumah   I'm the same person.

Dorman   Why are you acting like this? It's like you don't even like me anymore. I thought we had something special.

Nkrumah   This is not the right place to talk.

Dorman   I didn't make things up in my head about us, Kwame. You've been kissing me for months /

Nkrumah   Lower your voice /

Dorman   I've been there for you. /

Nkrumah   Betty, my work is my only focus. (*Beat.*) I don't want any unnecessary distractions.

Beat.

Dorman   Go to hell, Kwame!

Dorman *returns to* **Johnson**. *She's upset.* **Ashwood Garvey**
returns.

Ashwood Garvey   Who mek di white girl cry? /

Johnson (*to* **Nkrumah**)   Right. I've had enough of you. Outside.

Dorman   Len, leave it. It's not worth it.

Kenyatta   No brawling in or outside the club. They'll call the police on us /

La Badie *laughs to herself.* **Dorman** *notices.*

Dorman   What are you laughing at?

La Badie   Excuse me? /

Dorman   You laughed at me.

Kenyatta   Betty, she's not laughing at you. /

La Badie *scoffs again.*

Dorman   She just did it again, Jomo /

La Badie   She has a name. /

Dorman (*to* **La Badie**)   You've been watching me all night, *Alma.*

La Badie   I've been watching everybody.

Pizer   Betty, please calm down. /

Dorman   She's the one with the problem, Dorothy. /

La Badie (*to* **Dorman**)   You like this, don't you? These men fighting over you. /

Nkrumah   I'm not fighting over her /

Dorman (*to* **La Badie**   Are you jealous of me or something? (**La Badie** *laughs.*) You see me with Len. You don't like it. You see me with Kwame. You don't like it. You see me with Joe. You don't like it. You see me with Marko. You don't like it. They're *my* friends. She's just shown up here. This is *my* city! /

Pizer   It's our city /

La Badie   I don't need to be here long to see what you're after /

Dorman   What are you implying? /

Ashwood Garvey   That you're a Jezebel, darling /

Kenyatta   Amy?! /

Dorman (*to* **Ashwood Garvey**)   I've been working for the Congress just like everyone else. I'm allowed to have a good time too /

La Badie   When women like you have a good time it's dangerous. /

Dorman   Dangerous? /

La Badie   Your desires are dangerous /

Dorman   You don't know what I desire. /

Ashwood Garvey   So why yuh boo boo crying ova Kwame?! /

Dorman   That's no one's business.

La Badie   Until your stomach starts to swell and your mother has the BPP smashing windows and calling you all niggerlovers. (*Beat.*) Will you claim these men as your friends then? (*Beat.*) Or will you dump your coloured baby at my church before your family finds out?

Dorman   You don't know anything about my family. They would welcome any child I have. /

Pizer   Giving your life to men like Kwame is not the same as committing to some boy from Hulme. /

La Badie   Women like you can't handle a fraction of the contempt and disgust the world dishes out on us daily. (*Beat.*) The second you're threatened with disownment you'll throw away your coloured baby and erase your black dalliance from your memory. (*She turns to* **Kenyatta**.) And you all let her do it.

Kenyatta   What have I done?

She looks at **Nkrumah**.

La Badie   You black men who chase and choose and give permission to these white women to be comfortable around us. These women have no idea of what it means to truly love you. (*Beat.*) They confuse the pleasure of you entering them as knowing your black body. (*Beat.*) They know lust. (*Beat.*) They know curiosity. (*Steps closer to* **Nkrumah**.) But let me ask you, can she see your wounds? (*Beat.*) Can she hold your fears? (*Beat.*) Can she protect you?

(*Beat. He doesn't answer.*)

Dorman   Kwame? /

La Badie   Then, how'd you trust her to birth your black child? (*Beat.*) Being African matters so much to you that you're willing to risk your life by returning home to liberate it. (*Beat.*) But you leave these black babies to grow up with only a tale of a good time as the only explanation of their existence. (*Beat.*) They'll never find protection in their mother's race and citizenship. /

Dorman   I'd make sure they would. /

La Badie   They'll be haunted by the ghost of a black father. (*Turns to* **Nkrumah**.) Manchester is an annotation in the full Kwame Nkrumah story. (*Beat.*) So why leave such a trail of destruction? (*She turns to* **Dorman**.) Unless, you're willing to leave Manchester too? To stand beside him in the Gold Coast to fight as dissidents against your empire. (*Beat.*) They arrest and torture traitors. Can you see yourself sitting on a wet concrete prison floor for decades, Betty?

The room waits for **Dorman** *to answer.* **Dorman** *waits for them to defend her.*

Silence. **Ashwood Garvey** *starts clapping.*

Ashwood Garvey   Well done, Alma! (*She gets up and hugs her.*) That's my girl!

La Badie *is emotionally drained. She pulls away from* **Ashwood Garvey** *and exits.*

Pizer   Let's all call it a night.

Pizer *and* **Ashwood Garvey** *exit.* **Kenyatta** *alone.*

Kenyatta (*to himself*)   And I'm the one George says needs chaperoning.

Kenyatta *sucks his teeth. He turns off the sign and exits.*

Scene Two

On the Same Team

Day 5: Friday 19 October 1945, morning.

Pizer *and* **Padmore** *kitchen.*

A projection:

'DAY 5: FRIDAY 19 OCTOBER 1945'

Lights up on **Padmore** *sitting at a dining table with a typewriter and a pile of blank papers. His suit jacket and tie hang on a chair. His shirt sleeves are rolled up. Shirt buttons open.*

'COLONIAL AND COLOURED UNITY: A PROGRAMME OF ACTION.

A PAN-AFRICAN MANIFESTO

EDITED BY . . .'

He stops. He pulls out the paper from the typewriter and throws it away. He types again. A projection:

'COLONIAL AND COLOURED UNITY: A PROGRAMME OF ACTION.

A HISTORY OF THE PAN-AFRICAN CONGRESS

EDITED BY

GEORGE PADMORE.'

He pulls out the paper and sets it aside. The projection ends. **Pizer** *enters dressed in a night gown.*

Padmore   I've started drafting but I think I need to reorder the sections. I removed 'manifesto' from the cover, it felt too confronting, or maybe it should be? I don't know. Can you take a look? (*She starts making herself a cup of tea.*) Maybe Du Bois' final remarks will give it a better structure. (*Beat.*) I forgot to ask him for a copy. He was already falling asleep by the time I was leaving him his accommodation. He started muttering something about his father, I didn't know if he was still talking to me or had started dreaming. (*He starts doing up his shirt and putting on his tie.*) He said, 'My daddy left the family, and now I'm a father to congresses'. (*Beat.*) Imagine, this elderly man is still that little boy waiting on his father to come home. (*Beat.*) The journalist in me wanted to pry further. Do you think his father regrets leaving his son, given what Du Bois has become? (*Beat.* **Pizer** *doesn't respond. She sips her tea.*) Dorothy, did you hear me?

Beat.

Pizer   I heard you, George.

He notices her energy is low. Beat.

Padmore   Did you have a good time last night?

Beat.

Pizer   Yes.

Beat.

Padmore   You should get dressed. We'll be late.

Pizer   I'll be there in the tea break.

Padmore   Why?

She looks up.

Pizer   George, no one is going to miss me for a couple of hours.

Padmore   I will. Are you sick?

She continues making her breakfast. Beat.

Pizer   No.

Padmore   Has something happened?

Pizer   No.

Padmore   So, what's the matter?

Pizer   Let's talk about it after the Congress. /

Padmore   No. Let's talk about it now /

Pizer   They're my feelings, George. I'll decide when we talk about them. /

Padmore   It's the last day of the Congress, you can't take the morning off. /

Pizer   I'm not a machine, George. (*Beat.*) I just need the morning.

Padmore   If you need extra help, I can get Betty to do it. It'll distract her from kissing Kwame.

Pizer   I didn't tell you about them kissing for you to embarrass her. I can handle my work. /

Padmore   So what's the problem then?!

Pizer   Pour l'amour de Dieu, George (For God's sake, George) /

Padmore   You're speaking in French so I know you're upset. (*Beat.*) Have I angered you? /

Pizer   Do you see me as your family, George?

Beat.

Padmore   What?

Beat.

Pizer   I understand the work we do. (*Beat.*) We met each other doing this work. It is a big part of our intimacy. But, we are still two people in this. Right?

Padmore   Right.

Pizer   But what do I mean to you? It's been ten years. Everyone calls me your wife. (*Beat.*) But I'm not. /

Padmore   Do you want to get married? /

Pizer   No /

Padmore   Then what are we talking about?

Beat.

Pizer   Julia married Malcolm. (*Beat.*) I met George. (*Beat.*) They are not the same man.

Padmore   And you're not the same women.

Pause.

Pizer   George, do you love *me* or am I someone who introduced you to Communist party members when you arrived in England? Someone that transcribes manuscripts, does your French translations, proofreads, hosts your friends, hosts your mentees, and pays all the bills when you need to write.

Padmore   I lived off my writing before I met you. But it sounds like I've been incurring debts I wasn't aware off. /

Pizer   Don't insult me /

Padmore   Where's all this coming from?

Beat.

Pizer   Kwame said, /

Padmore   What did he say?!

Beat.

Pizer   Do you ever wish you could go back to being Malcolm again? (*Beat.*) Go back to Trinadad, be married to Julia ?

Beat.

Padmore   There is no going back. /

Pizer   But if you could? /

Padmore   Dorothy, I was always going to become this man.
I may not have the words to describe this life, but I was a
young boy writing about injustice for the local paper, long
before I married Julia. (*Beat*.) You know this.

Pizer   I know that I feel distant from you. (*Beat*.) Kwame
has had access to you and what's going on in here (*Places her
hand on his chest*.) more than I have for months. (*Beat*.) You
told him that you regret not being there for Blyden's life.

Beat.

Padmore   Kwame caught me in a drunken moment.

Beat.

Pizer   But still a moment of truth. (*Beat*.) Talk to me,
George.

Pause.

Padmore   It wasn't just Blyden I was thinking about. (*Beat*.)
Everyone expects something different from me. (*Beat*.)
Father, husband, leader, radical, Communist, journalist,
(*Beat*.) I don't know if I have enough years for all these
duties.

Pizer   Why didn't you tell me you were feeling this way?

Pause.

Padmore   It's because it's you. (*Beat*.) Your love strips me
naked. (*Beat*.) No armour. Just flesh (*Beat*.) Fragile. (*Beat*.)
You soften parts of me. (*Beat*.) Your love reminds me that I
can die. (*Beat*.) I can't think when my heart is racing, and it
feels like there's no air in the room. The Congress doesn't
need that version of me. (*Beat*.) They need me to be steady.
To be focused. We don't know how long this window will be
open. /

Pizer   But *this* week was a success /

Padmore   My notes are still disjointed and they're all leaving tonight. They need a manifesto that will make an impact that lasts for generations.

Pizer   George, you've already done so much /

Padmore   It's not enough! (*Beat.*) How many pamphlets, organisations, forums, protests and rallies have we done together in the last decade? (*Beat.*) But still, so much needs to change. (*Beat.*) We cut one head off the Hydra and it grows another more mutated, more vicious, more fascist. (*Beat.*) I'm constantly trying to figure out how I replenish with new weapons and new armies /

Pizer   Isn't this why we welcome the mentees? (*Beat.*) To train them. /

Padmore   I've been trying to do that with Kwame but he's so impatient. /

Pizer   Like you were?

Padmore   He's nothing like me. He wants everything now.

Beat.

Pizer   Like you once did? /

Padmore   And where did that get me? (*Beat.*) Hopeful that the white allies in Hamburg would always show me their support. But when the Nazis came into power and ransacked my offices, where was the Communist Party? (*Beat.*) Protecting their financial interests whilst sacrificing me. I was lucky the Nazis, only exiled me. (*Beat.*) I don't want that for Kwame. /

Pizer   You can't protect him from everything /

Padmore   I want him to have people he trusts. I want him to have strategy. I'm trying to set the pace for him, but he wants to sprint through a marathon. (*Beat.*) He infuriates me. /

Pizer   You've had difficult mentees before. This isn't new for you. /

Padmore   But it's never been like this, Dorothy. At this point in history, when we might have a real chance for independence. (*Beat.*) Kwame is so determined to be president that I don't know if I genuinely believe he can do it. (*Beat.*) If I could jump time, I wouldn't go back. I'd go forward to see what he does, then I'd know if he's worth the effort.

Pizer   He is.

Beat.

Padmore   How'd you know?

Pizer   Because there are queues of people wanting your mentorship; and we're still talking about Kwame. (*Beat.*) I saw you watching him yesterday. You want him to come back to you.

Beat.

Padmore   He called me a dimming flame, Dorothy. (*Beat.*) Other mentees wouldn't dare.

Pizer   Maybe he's more than a mentee.

Padmore   He's not my friend.

Beat.

Pizer   He didn't leave. (*Beat.*) He's not done learning, and you're not done teaching.

Padmore   He won't be easy to guide. It might take years. (*Beat.*) Are you sure you want to put up with me for a bit longer?

Beat.

Pizer   Jusqu'à ce que la mort nous sépare.

Padmore   Till death do us part.

They kiss and exit.

Scene Three

Black Woman to Black Woman

Day 5: Friday 19 October 1945, afternoon.

All Saint's Church grounds, afternoon.

La Badie *enters and crosses the stage.* **Johnson** *follows behind her.*

Johnson   Alma, wait. Where've you been all day?

La Badie   I don't want to talk to you, Len. /

Johnson   Why? Are you alright?

She stops and turns to him.

La Badie   You're asking now? You didn't care last night when you left.

Johnson   Betty was upset. I couldn't let her walk home alone.

La Badie   Ain't I a woman too? /

Johnson   Yes you are /

La Badie   I need protecting in these streets /

Johnson   And I would have run out after you if you'd left first. I'm your friend too. /

La Badie   Dorothy spoke up more than you did last night /

Johnson   That's not fair, Alma! /

La Badie   It's not fair always being the one calling out people's hypocrisy /

Johnson   Some of the things you were saying last night weren't as black and white to me. (*Beat.*) I felt like I was caught in-between. Since I was a kid, no matter what I say, where I go, what choose someone is going to be upset. (*Beat.*) Last night, I was trying to figure out where I fit in what you were saying (*Beat.*) When I met Maria she already had three white children. Now that her sister's passed, I've adopted three more. I've wondered if people see me as a hypocrite. Fighting racism but look at the family I've got (*Beat.*) It's not lost on me that I am a coloured man in a world that sees his children and wife as more human than him. (*Beat.*) My kids are young. I want to teach my kids to be decent people. To learn to see humanity like Marko says. (*Beat.* **Ashwood Garvey** *enters behind* **La Badie**. *She lingers and listens.*) Betty is doing the opposite. She is unlearning how she was raised. She means well but there's things she still doesn't see. (*Beat.*) I can help with that. Dorothy can help. (*Beat.*) I should have said that last night, but you're faster and shaper with words than my right hook. /

Ashwood Garvey   Alma is a lethal woman. Len, can I talk to Alma alone please?

La Badie (*to* **Ashwood Garvey**)   I don't have the strength to talk to you right now.

La Badie *turns to leave.*

Ashwood Garvey   If you walk away, Alma, I'm going to chase you. (*Beat.*) Let me say what I need to, and if you have nothing to add, you can go.

La Badie *turns back.*

La Badie   Fine.

Ashwood Garvey   Len, can you give us a moment.

Johnson *nods and exits.*

Ashwood Garvey   Please sit. (**La Badie** *remains standing. Beat.*) You didn't come to my talk this morning. (*Beat.*) I wished you had. (*Beat.*) I praised how you earned your delegates pin all on your own.

La Badie   If I'd known George's invitation letter was laced with so many false promises, I wouldn't have come.

Ashwood Garvey   You're disappointed with what you found here?

La Badie   With whom. I see all your contradictions.

Ashwood Garvey   That's people, Alma.

La Badie   We're supposed to be better.

Ashwood Garvey   Why?

Beat.

La Badie   Do you really want me to answer that?

Ashwood Garvey   Alma, the stories your mother told you about me are all true. I've done great things. But you're a big woman now. See me with your own eyes. (*Beat.*) I am not perfect. I never said I was. I have rough edges that cut. /

La Badie   I don't have to accept that being repeatedly cut and dismissed and ignored, by everyone, especially not by my own people. My parents raised me to value myself and others. /

Ashwood Garvey   You left your mother's house, by choice. Now you're angry the world isn't coddling you? (*Beat.*) Yes, Alma, it is hard out here. (*Beat.*) So what do you want to do about it?

Pause. **La Badie** *sits.*

La Badie   I trained as a social worker because I wanted to take care of my community. (*Beat.*) But I started this week, as an undertaker for another black child. I sat in sessions after sessions, hearing of all the injustices in the colonies to then look around a room full of egos. (*Beat.*) The last bit of my faith in us burned to ash last night. (*Beat.*) I've been stopping here on my lunch breaks. I keep hearing my mother saying, when you're in pain go to God. (*Beat.*) But somehow, these church ruins speak more clearly to me now than the standing building ever did. (*Beat.*) I keep swallowing pain, and people expect me to still teach, and still love, and defend and dream. If my hands are full, no one is patting my back. /

Ashwood Garvey   Who did you expect to? /

La Badie   You! (*Beat.*) I expected you to. (*Beat.*) I'm not strong enough to endure being cut or to do this work alone. (*Beat.*) I won't survive, and the weight of my falling body will crush every black girl coming up under me. (*Beat.*) I want to pat her back too. (*Beat.*) I want to hug her. (*Beat.*) I want to let her cry. (*Beat.*) And maybe that's too soft for you, but softness and love should be in the manifesto too. Let me be remembered for that, instead of being like you.

Pause. **Ashwood Garvey** *takes out the 'CHAIRMAN' sign from her handbag.*

Ashwood Garvey   Here. Take this. /

La Badie   Everyone is looking for that /

Ashwood Garvey   Take this.

La Badie   I can't take that. /

Ashwood Garvey   Yes you can. /

La Badie   It doesn't belong to me /

Ashwood Garvey   I'm Chairman. It belongs to me, now I'm giving it to you. Take it. (*Beat.*) Pass this on to the next girl. (*Beat.*) You can be a better mentor than I was.

Beat. **La Badie** *takes the sign. She suddenly hugs* **Ashwood Garvey** *tightly.* **Ashwood Garvey** *is taken aback. It takes her a moment to return the affection. They hold each other.*

La Badie   Thank you.

Ashwood Garvey *pulls back.*

Ashwood Garvey   Okay, okay. That's enough.

Pizer *enters.*

Pizer   Amy, we're heading over to the restaurant.

Ashwood Garvey   Right behind you, Dorothy. (**Pizer** *exits.*) Share your proposal with everyone, Alma. (*She gets up to leave.*) And they're taking final pictures of everyone later.

Make sure you get yours done. The future must know Alma La Badie was here.

La Badie *nods and exits.*

Scene Four

Declarations

Day 5: Friday 19 October 1945, afternoon.

Forum Restaurant.

The FORUM RESTURANT sign is turned on. **Ashwood Garvey** *is joined by* **Kenyatta**, **Padmore** *and* **Pizer**. **Padmore** *enters carrying a stack of papers. He hands out copies to them all.*

Padmore   Obviously it's not a complete list of resolutions. But from transcribing some the rapporteurs' notes, our demands break down into three categories: political, economic and social. (*Beat.*) I think every region of the continent should have its own declarations. And at the back we should also include the letters of support we've received. I've put Mr Surat Ali's letter from the Federation of Indian Association of Great Britain as an example. (*Beat.*) Also, it is imperative that we show our solidarity to other struggling peoples. I have been keeping up with the reports coming out of Indonesia and Vietnam. They're taking up arms against the Dutch and French.

Kenyatta   It's a good start, George.

Pizer   Did you speak to Du Bois?

Padmore   Yes, he gave me an advanced copy of his final remarks. (*He takes out a piece of paper and hands it to her.*)

His handwriting is cursive. It needs deciphering.

Pizer   I'll type it up.

Kenyatta   May I have a look?

Pizer *hands him the paper.*

Padmore   His presence really lifted morale (*Beat.*) It's a shame someone tried to ruin it by stealing the chairman sign.

Ashwood Garvey, **Pizer** *and* **Kenyatta** *exchange smiles.*

Ashwood Garvey   Scoundrels!

Beat.

Kenyatta   Du Bois is asking how we are going to govern ourselves once we leave. (*Beat.*) My dear friends, we have made it to the final day. Looking around this restaurant, which delegate would you pass the baton to? /

Ashwood Garvey   I nominate myself.

Kenyatta   You can't nominate yourself. /

Ashwood Garvey   All the promises aren't solely in the young, Jomo. You are an ambassador for the Kikuyu people. They would rally if you called for a republic.

Kenyatta   I'm already fifty-four, I maybe have twenty good years left in me. These resolutions need more decades to implement. (*He scans the room.*) Who would you pick? (*They all scan the audience. Beat.*) I say Marko. (*They laugh.*) Art is powerful and lives on after death. /

Ashwood Garvey   And artists love attention. He'll get too distracted and make his movie premiers national holidays.

Pizer   We need someone here, when everyone goes back home. So, my money's on Len. He's already a well-known name.

Ashwood Garvey   Alma is focused too. (*Beat.*) She's already building traction in England and worked as a clerk for the Jamaican government. She has a good heart and understands the bureaucracies of high office.

Beat.

Pizer   Isn't anyone going to say Betty?

They all laugh.

Ashwood Garvey   That one still needs to go through the Dorothy Pizer, Finishing School of Allyship.

Pizer   Don't worry, I've enrolled her already.

Kenyatta   Joseph has a legal background. I can see him going into politics once he graduates.

Pizer   That's if Kwame doesn't eat his competition first.

Kenyatta   You're quiet, George. (*Beat.*) What's your verdict on your boy?

Pause.

Padmore   There could be a president once I'm done with him.

Kenyatta   But be careful, my friend, there is no putting old heads on young shoulders. (*Beat.*) We were young once. We forged our own paths too. (*Beat.*) Kwame clearly doesn't want to be moulded into a copy of you. (*Beat.*) We must see who these young people are. (*Beat.*) Peter turned one in August. (*Beat.*) I look at my son and I wonder what world he will inherit. (*Beat.*) Will my oppressor still be his oppressor? (*Beat.*) My culture anchors me in this world, but he might grow to think of himself as English as Edna. (*Beat.*) He is different from my other children back home with Grace. (*Beat.*) Muigai and Margaret are Kikuyu. (*Beat.*) Do I love them more because they resemble my skin and speak my mother tongue? (*Beat.*) They are all my children. (*Beat.*) They all look at me and call me father. (*Beat.*) We must see our nations the same way. Homes filled with different children that all require parenting. (*Beat. Refers to the papers in his hands.*) Du Bois says we will make mistakes. (*Beat.*) We have a right to when building new nations; but not the audacity to act like we never make mistakes. (*Beat.*) That will only condemn us.

Ashwood Garvey   And God forbid they are all back here in another in fifty, eighty, or a hundred years saying these declarations never came to pass.

Kenyatta   The white man will only continue growing fatter if he is feasting on our disunity. (*Beat.*) So, we need to know, George, did you make any mistakes with Kwame?

Silence. **Padmore** *sighs deeply. Lights down on them.* **Appiah** *and* **Hlubi** *enter. They're followed by* **Nkrumah**.

Nkrumah   Joe, Marko, please. Can we talk?

Hlubi   What do you want?

Nkrumah (*pulls them aside*)   Can we?

Appiah   You don't want George to see you?

Nkrumah   I don't want to talk by the entrance of the restaurant.

Beat. They stand in silence for a moment.

Appiah   Go on.

Beat.

Nkrumah   Listen, I took out some things on you.

Appiah   And George and Betty and Jomo and Len /

Nkrumah   God, you will never take it easy on me.

Appiah   Never.

Nkrumah   Noted. (*Beat.*) The knots of wisdom are untying themselves, slowly.

Appiah   Thank you for admitting I'm always right /

Nkrumah   I didn't say that /

Appiah   I'm a natural born leader. /

Nkrumah   Can I take back my apology?

They laugh. **Hlubi** *doesn't join in. Beat.*

Hlubi   I've not actually heard an apology.

There's a tension between them. Beat.

Nkrumah   Your art matters, Marko.

Hlubi   I know.

Beat.

Nkrumah   I'm sorry. (*Beat.*) I'm trying to figure out what you've already done for yourself. (**Nkrumah** *holds out his hand.*) Friends?.

Beat.

Hlubi   Good luck with your quest, Kwame.

Hlubi *exits. Beat.*

Appiah   Give him time.

Nkrumah   We're out of time.

Beat.

Appiah   At least smooth things out with George before we leave.

Beat.

Nkrumah   Yes, boss!

La Badie *enters and walks past them towards the restaurant.*

Nkrumah (*calls out*)   So, how many times can we redo a first impression?

She turns back.

La Badie   The answer is in the description.

Nkrumah   Give us a minute, Joe.

Appiah (*to* **Nkrumah**)   I'll see you back at the town hall. (*To* **La Badie**.) Good afternoon, Miss Alma.

La Badie   Afternoon, Joe.

Appiah *exits. Beat.*

Nkrumah   I've run out of time to change your mind about me.

La Badie   Maybe, one day you might do something great and, I'll read about you and feel proud I once met you (*Beat.*) or maybe not.

He laughs.

Nkrumah   I deserve that. (*Beat.*) Or maybe it's you, I'll read about in all the history books, and I'll just be a footnote. (*Beat.*) An almost somebody.

Beat.

La Badie   That's a lot of maybes.

Nkrumah   Still, no matter where we go in the world, we're connected. We'll always have Manchester.

Beat.

La Badie   Was it worth coming for you?

Padmore *exits the restaurant and runs into* **Nkrumah** *and* **La Badie**. *Beat.*

Nkrumah (*to Ladie*)   We'll see.

La Badie *nods and exits.*

Scene Five

Legacy

Day 5: 19 October 1945, afternoon

Forum Restaurant.

Nkrumah   I stayed.

Beat.

Padmore   I see.

Padmore *maintains eye contact. Silence.*

Nkrumah   You are not going to jump in to fill the silence, are you?

Beat.

Padmore   No.

Beat.

Nkrumah   I'm not sorry for what I said. (*Beat.*) But I could have raised my concerns in private. (*Beat.*) Or less reactively.

Padmore   My door has always been open.

Nkrumah   Except the other ninety percent of the time when it's closed. (*Beat.*) You're an as open as you think you are, George.

Beat.

Padmore   I've been told I can be a little, distant /

Nkrumah   An enigma. A contradiction. A paradox. A mystification /

Padmore   Enough.

Beat.

Nkrumah   You treated me like a colleague for months, until you finally invited me into your home. But I still felt like a spectator around your friends, and then suddenly one night you got personal. /

Padmore   I didn't mean to /

Nkrumah   But I thought great, he's letting me in. He trusts me. We're becoming friends. But then, you caught yourself, built your walls back up, this time much higher and thicker and meaner. (*Beat.*) How could I come to you? (*Beat.*) You know I came here for you. (*Beat.*) I had something to prove but you've been shutting me down for a while. (*Beat.*) This is not the great George Padmore I expected.

Beat.

Padmore I am simply a man, Nkrumah. /

Nkrumah You're a man who leads with composure and everyone's respect. I want that for myself. But . . .

Beat.

Padmore But what?

Pause.

Nkrumah I am not composed inside. (*Beat.*) Everything I feel quickly turns into a hurricane.

Padmore Your rage made a wreck this week.

Nkrumah My rage has been picking up speed for a while. (*Beat.*) I'm afraid . . .

Pause.

Padmore What are you afraid of?

Pause.

Nkrumah What if I go back home and I'm not enough for my people?

Pause.

Padmore Are you enough for yourself?

Pause.

Nkrumah I used to see greatness in the mirror. (*Beat.*) But lately, I see a blur. (*Beat.*) How do you carry it all?

Beat.

Padmore Who says I do?

Nkrumah It's what it looks like from the outside.

Padmore I have my own fears.

Nkrumah *waits for* **Padmore** *to elaborate. He doesn't.*

Nkrumah   You keep saying we don't have time. Africa needs liberating now. How do we do that if we can't speak to each other honestly? (*Beat.*) I want to learn from you George. But if I can't access you, your mentorship becomes an obstacle that I must go through /

Padmore   And if you keep with that mentality, one day you will find an obstacle you can't go through. (*Beat.*) It will go through you. An abduction. A noose. A prison. A bullet. (*Beat.*) These governments will kill you. (*Beat.*) I'm trying to keep you alive for as long as possible to make change happen. (*Beat.*) I want to see you do that /

Nkrumah   I feel all the responsibility of that. (*Beat.*) I want to be a great leader. I don't want to be the reason why my people have more grief than hope for generations to come.

Pause. **Padmore** *steps closer to* **Nkrumah**.

Padmore   To liberate anyone, you must first overthrow what you fear within yourself, Nkrumah. (*Beat.*) It was never going to happen over one week in Manchester. (*Beat.*) It is your life's work.

Beat.

Nkrumah   But what if along the way I don't run like you do? (*Beat.*) What if I want to veer off your path and carve out a different way. (*Beat.*) Will you threaten to quit on me again?

Pause.

Padmore   We can map out your journey, together.

Beat. **Nkrumah** *smiles.*

Nkrumah   Can I co-edit the manifesto? /

Padmore   No. (*Beat.*) I will handle that. Everyone will get their credits.

Pause.

Nkrumah   Do you feel it?

Padmore   What?

Nkrumah   The new shift in our relationship.

Padmore   I'm spoken for, Nkrumah.

Nkrumah   Joint Secretaries was fun. Mentor and mentee feels junior now.

Padmore   We're not becoming friends. Let's go hear Du Bois' closing. /

They start walking together.

Nkrumah   I was going to say brothers. /

Padmore   I already have a brother /

Nkrumah   You do? (*Beat.*) What's his name? Do you like him more than me?

Padmore   Please tone down your theatrics before you become president.

Nkrumah   My personality is my charm.

Padmore   We'll see.

Nkrumah *stops* **Padmore**.

Nkrumah   How about, George Padmore, the Adviser for African Affairs to the President of the Gold Coast, Kwame Nkrumah.

Beat.

Padmore   Get elected first.

Nkrumah *holds out his hand. Beat.* **Padmore** *shakes it. All delegates flood the stage.*

Congress portraits

Nkrumah *and* **Padmore** *pose together. Camera flashes.* **Padmore** *steps away.*

La Badie *joins* **Nkrumah**. *They pose together. Camera flashes.*
Appiah *joins them. They pose together. Camera flashes.*

Johnson *hovers.* **Nkrumah** *steps away.* **La Badie** *holds out her hand to* **Johnson**. *Beat. He hugs her. Camera flashes. Hlubi joins them.* **La Badie**, **Johnson**, **Appiah** *and* **Hlubi** *pose. Camera flashes.*

Dorman *joins them.* **La Badie** *steps away.* **Dorman**, **Appiah** *and* **Hlubi** *pose. Camera flashes.*

Ashwood Garvey *pulls* **La Badie** *back to centre stage.* **Ashwood Garvey** *and* **La Badie** *pose. Camera flashes.* **La Badie** *steps away.*

Appiah *quickly rushes over to get a picture with* **Ashwood Garvey**. *Camera flashes. He steps away.*

Pizer *joins* **Ashwood Garvey**. *They pose together. Camera flashes.* **Ashwood Garvey** *steps away.*

Pizer *beckons* **Dorman** *to join her. They pose together. Camera flashes.* **Dorman** *steps away.*

Kenyatta *joins* **Pizer**. *He dips her. Camera flashes.* **Padmore** *pulls* **Kenyatta** *away from* **Pizer**. *Camera flashes.*

All the delegates pose together. Camera flashes.

Blackout.

*9 781350 586468 *